BREAKING ~~DOWN~~ THROUGH

A JOURNEY THROUGH MEDICINE,
ONE CHAPTER AT A TIME

DR. YASHASWI GUNTUPALLI

BREAKING ~~DOWN~~ THROUGH

A JOURNEY THROUGH MEDICINE,
ONE CHAPTER AT A TIME

DR. YASHASWI GUNTUPALLI

Dr. Yashaswi Guntupalli

Dr. Madhulika Chaudhury

By Dr. Darshini Kattula

Dr.Gowrava Vijayalakshmi

Dr. Arpitha Sirichandana Baggu

Dr. Vijetha Reddy Katta

Dr. P Sri Sai Githa

Dr. Prashasti Sharma

Dr. Bonny Rishitha Beeda

Dr. Sarakinti Sarika

Dr. Venkata Sai Deepthi Rayadurgam

Dr. Yuvakeerthana Ramachandra

Dr. A R Chaitanya

Dr. Shriramya. M

Dr. Sree Sritha Nellore

Dr. S. Sreeja

Dr. Sujani Raja

Dr. Shrishti P. Khetan

Dr. Shruti Suresh Suvarna

INDIA • SINGAPORE • MALAYSIA

Epigraph

"The life so short, the craft so long to learn."
— *Hippocrates*

Dedication

"To every student who has stepped into the world of medicine–
With a heart full of dreams and a mind full of doubts,
To the ones who walked this path with me—
To the sleepless nights and early morning rounds,
To the bonds forged in lecture halls and hospital corridors,
To the silent battles fought behind confident smiles,
To the ones who dreamed, struggled, and conquered—
To the professors who guided us,
To the patients who taught us,
To the friends who stood by us,
And to our families,
Whose unwavering support kept us going.
This book is for you."

CONTRIBUTING AUTHORS

Dr. Yashaswi Guntupalli, MBBS
SVIMS- Sri Padmavathi Medical College for Women, Tirupati, AP, India.

Dr. Madhulika Chaudhury, MBBS
SVIMS- Sri Padmavathi Medical College for Women, Tirupati, AP, India.

Dr. Darshini Kattula, MBBS
SVIMS- Sri Padmavathi Medical College for Women, Tirupati, AP, India.

Dr. Gowrava Vijayalakshmi, MBBS
SVIMS- Sri Padmavathi Medical College for Women, Tirupati, AP, India.

Dr. Arpitha Sirichandana Baggu, MBBS
SVIMS- Sri Padmavathi Medical College for Women, Tirupati, AP, India.

Dr. Vijetha Reddy Katta, MBBS
SVIMS- Sri Padmavathi Medical College for Women, Tirupati, AP, India.

Dr. P Sri Sai Githa, MBBS
SVIMS- Sri Padmavathi Medical College for Women, Tirupati, AP, India.

Dr. Prashasti Sharma, MBBS
SVIMS- Sri Padmavathi Medical College for Women, Tirupati, AP, India.

Dr. Bonny Rishitha Beeda, MBBS
SVIMS- Sri Padmavathi Medical College for Women, Tirupati, AP, India.

Dr. Sarakinti Sarika, MBBS
SVIMS- Sri Padmavathi Medical College for Women, Tirupati, AP, India.

Dr. Venkata Sai Deepthi Rayadurgam, MBBS
SVIMS- Sri Padmavathi Medical College for Women, Tirupati, AP, India.

Dr. Yuvakeerthana Ramachandra, MBBS
SVIMS- Sri Padmavathi Medical College for Women, Tirupati, AP, India.

Dr. A R Chaitanya, MBBS, MD
MD Pulmonary Medicine; fellowship - Diploma in Asthma and Allergy (CMC VELLORE), Ex-assistant professor (SVIMS), India.

Dr. Shriramya. M, MBBS, MD
MBBS (JIPMER), MD Medicine (SVIMS), Fellowship in Diabetology, India.

Dr. Sree Sritha, Nellore, MBBS
SVIMS- Sri Padmavathi Medical College for Women, Tirupati, AP, India.

Dr. S. Sreeja, MBBS
SVIMS- Sri Padmavathi Medical College for Women, Tirupati, AP, India.

Dr. Sujani Raja, MBBS
SVIMS- Sri Padmavathi Medical College for Women, Tirupati, AP, India.

Dr. Shrishti P. Khetan, MD, MHA,
American University of Barbados, Wildey, Saint Michael, Barbados.

Dr. Shruti Suresh Suvarna, MD, MHA
American University of Barbados, Wildey, Saint Michael, Barbados.

CONTENTS

PREFACE

edicine is not just a career; it is a calling, a journey of discovery, and a lifelong commitment to learning. The path to becoming a doctor is paved with long nights, difficult lessons, and moments of self-doubt. Yet, it is also filled with friendships, victories, and profound experiences that shape us into the healers we aspire to be.

"Breaking ~~Down~~ Through" is a collection of 22 chapters, each written by a different voice, chronicling the highs and lows of medical school. As the chief author and compiler, I have poured not only my own experiences but also the heartfelt stories of my peers into these pages. My journey, filled with its own challenges and triumphs, is interwoven with those of countless others who dared to dream of making a difference.

This book is not just about the struggles—it is about resilience, the laughter shared in hospital corridors, the lessons learned from patients, and the moments that make it all worthwhile.

To every medical student and doctor who has ever questioned their place in this journey—this book is a reminder that you are never alone.

ACKNOWLEDGEMENTS

Bringing this book to life has been a journey in itself, and I am deeply grateful to everyone who made it possible.

To my co-authors—your willingness to share your experiences, honesty, and unique perspectives have created something truly special. Your voices make this book a meaningful reflection of the medical journey.

To the mentors and professors who guided us—not just in academics, but in the art of medicine itself—your wisdom and support have been invaluable.

To my family and friends—your patience, unwavering support, encouragement, and belief in me have made all the difference. A special thank you to my mom, dad, sister, and the rest of my family, as well as my best friend—your endless love, faith, and unwavering support have been my guiding light through every challenge.

And most importantly, to the readers—thank you for allowing us to share our journey with you. May these stories inspire and reassure you, just as they did for us while writing them.

Finally, to every medical student who picks up this book—I hope you find a piece of yourself in these pages. Thank you for being part of this story.

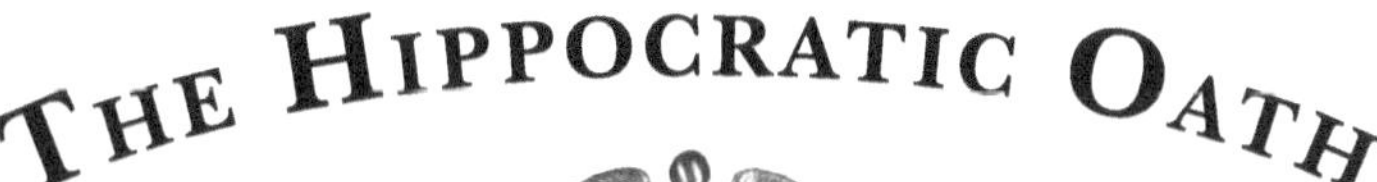THE HIPPOCRATIC OATH

...I SWEAR ...

in the presence of the Almighty and before my family, my teachers, and my peers that according to my ability and judgement I will keep this oath and stipulation.

...TO RECOGNIZE...

all who have taught me this art, equally dear to me as my parents and in the same spirit and dedication to impart a knowledge of the art of medicine to others. I will continue with diligence to keep abreast of advances in medicine. I will treat without exception all who seek my ministrations, so long as the treatment of others is not compromised thereby, and I will seek the counsel of particularly skilled physicians where indicated for the benefit of my patient.

... I WILL FOLLOW...

that method of treatment which according to my ability and judgment, I consider for the benefit of my patient and abstain from whatever is harmful or mischievous. I will neither prescribe nor administer a lethal dose of medicine to any patient even if asked, nor counsel any such thing. I will hold the utmost respect for every human life from fertilization to natural death.

... WITH PURITY, HOLINESS AND BENEFICENCE ...

I will live my life and practice my art. Except for the prudent correction of an imminent danger, I will neither treat any patient nor carry out any research on any human being without the valid informed consent of the subject or the appropriate legal protector thereof, understanding that research must have as its purpose the furtherance of the health of that individual. Into whatever patient setting while I continue.

... TO KEEP THIS OATH...

may it be granted to me to enjoy life and the practice of the art and science of medicine with the blessing of the Almighty and respected by my peers and society, but should I trespass and violate this oath, may the reverse by my lot.

THE BEGINNING OF THE DREAM: MY FIRST YEAR JOURNEY

— *Dr. Yashaswi Guntupalli, MBBS,*
SVIMS- Sri Padmavathi Medical College for Women, Tirupati, AP, India.

*"Sometimes you will never know the value of a
moment until it becomes a memory."*

— *Dr. Seuss*

1

THE BEGINNING OF THE DREAM: MY FIRST YEAR JOURNEY

— Dr. Yashaswi Guntupalli, MBBS,
SVIMS- Sri Padmavathi Medical College for Women, Tirupati, AP, India.

The Moment It All Began

The moment I found out I had secured a seat in my college, my mind went blank. My parents, however, had a completely different reaction. "Yes, we did it! We don't have to look for any other options. It's God's own city. We are so lucky," they said, their voices filled with relief and excitement. I stood there, surprised and overwhelmed by a flood of emotions. Was I happy? Was I sad? I didn't know. I picked up my phone and called my best friends. "I got in," I told them, still trying to process everything. They cheered and congratulated me, but even their excitement couldn't drown out the thoughts creeping into my mind.

Then, the next morning, reality hit. Hard. I had to pack my bags and leave my home, my city, my comfort zone—to live in a new place all alone. "What will I even do?" I thought. My mind was a whirlwind of emotions.

A Women's College—But Why?

As I continued making calls to my friends, breaking the news to each of them, one of them asked, "Why a women's college?" Honestly? I had no answer. I never thought about it. It wasn't something I had considered deeply, yet here I was, heading toward a new chapter in a place I never specifically chose. And maybe that was okay. Maybe this was fate, or maybe it was just another part of the unknown I had to embrace.

The Long Road to Freedom

The hurdles before joining medical school felt insurmountable. Every exam, every sleepless night spent hunched over books, every whispered prayer—it felt as if the weight of the world rested squarely on my shoulders. But the moment I stepped into medical school, it was as though an enormous weight was lifted off my chest. I felt free—liberated—like I could finally breathe. Yet, deep down, I knew this was only the beginning. The road ahead would be steep and treacherous, littered with challenges far beyond what I had faced. What I didn't realize then was that the hurdles I had overcome weren't gone; they had merely transformed into something different.

Pride swelled within me the moment I secured my medical seat. For a fleeting time, it felt like I was on top of the world—like nothing could touch me. But as soon as I set foot on campus, that pride quickly gave way to humility. The realization struck me: I was surrounded by brilliant minds, all equally accomplished, if not more. The self-doubt crept in almost immediately. Was I really cut out for this? And most importantly, how would I find my place among strangers? Making friends had always seemed easy before, but now, it felt like a task I had to master anew.

Imposter Syndrome Creeps In

As the days went by, a strange feeling started settling in—something I didn't have a name for at the time but later recognized as **imposter syndrome**. Everyone around me seemed so sure, so confident. It felt like they belonged, like they knew exactly what they were doing. And then there was me, constantly wondering if I truly deserved to be here. Did I really earn this, or was it just luck? What if everyone realized I wasn't as smart as they thought? Would I be able to keep up with everyone else? These thoughts followed me like shadows, whispering doubts into my ears.

A New World, Far from Home

Leaving home for the first time and moving into a hostel was a bittersweet experience. I was thrilled by the thought of independence, of living in a new place, surrounded by people with the same aspirations. But the excitement was tinged with fear. Would I be able to adjust? Would I be homesick? The transition from the comfort of intermediate school to the vast, demanding world of MBBS was overwhelming. My familiar routines were replaced by an entirely new rhythm of life.

I missed home in ways I never expected. Festivals, once filled with laughter and togetherness, felt strangely empty without my family. I remember my first Holi away from home. While I longed for the traditions and warmth of celebrating with my loved ones, I found joy in an unexpected way—a Holi party organized with my batchmates. We danced all day with colors smeared across our faces, the music pounding, and laughter filling the air. For that brief moment, I felt truly alive, like I belonged. That day remains etched in my heart, a memory I hold close.

Yet, the ache of being away from home never fully disappeared. Nightly phone calls with my mom, dad, and sister became my anchor. No matter how hard the day had been, their voices brought me comfort and strength. My school best friends, though miles away, were there for me in ways I never imagined. Through a small device, my best friend became my lifeline, helping me navigate the lows and celebrating the highs. I longed for the days I could go home, but when I was home, I found myself missing the little freedoms and chaos of medical school. It was a strange paradox—being torn between two worlds, yet belonging fully to neither.

A Perfect Sunny Day, Yet a Storm Inside

After living in a hostel for 2 months, On one perfect sunny day—the kind where the warmth of the sun wasn't overbearing but just enough to make everything feel golden—I found myself standing on the Fifth floor of my hostel, staring at the hills in the distance. The view was breathtaking, but my mind wasn't taking in the beauty. All I could think about was, "How am I going to survive here without anyone?"

Back in 11th and 12th grade, I had lived in a hostel, but it was just twenty minutes away from home. I could go home every weekend, hug my parents, eat home-cooked meals, and recharge. It never felt like this. This was different. This was **an eight-hour drive away from home.** There were no weekend visits, no comfort of familiar streets or faces. Everything felt so foreign. I stood there, taking deep breaths, feeling a strange mix of fear, excitement, and uncertainty. I was clueless.

A Birthday to Remember

We joined medical school in late August. It took time for everyone to settle in, make friends, and adjust to this new life. Before we knew it, November had arrived. There had been a couple of birthdays before then, but mine, on the 10th of November, felt different. By this time, we had all grown close, and my birthday became the first one we truly celebrated together as a family.

Some of my friends locked me in my room while they secretly prepared for the celebration. They blew up balloons, bought a cake, and gathered party sprays and poppers. When it was finally time, they unlocked my door. As I stepped out, all the lights were off, replaced by the soft glow of candlelight, balloons floating around, and my friends standing everywhere, waiting. My phone rang with calls from my best friend and family back home, showering me with wishes.

I blew out the candle and laughed when I saw the cake—it had a girl holding a phone, a funny nod to the fact that I was always on my phone. Little did they know, I wasn't addicted to the device but to the people in it. The night was loud and filled with joy. Someone popped a balloon, and before we knew it, the warden arrived, warning us to quiet down. We hurriedly cleaned up and went to bed, but I drifted off to sleep feeling warm and happy. It was my first birthday away from home, yet my friends made sure I didn't miss it.

The next morning, I woke up feeling refreshed, dressed up, and headed to college. Then, out of nowhere, I got a call from the warden, asking me to report to the chief warden. Confused and unsure of what had happened, I went to her office. The moment I stepped in, she scolded me for the noise from the night before. I tried to explain that it was unintentional, just a birthday celebration, and that I hadn't planned it—my friends had surprised me. But she didn't listen. Instead, she called my parents and told them I was "involved in some things."

My parents, worried, called me immediately. I explained everything, and though they understood, they still apologized on my behalf. They even asked me to apologize, and I did. Tears rolled down my face—this was the first birthday where I had cried, and for no fault of mine. After everything, my chief warden unexpectedly handed me a pair of earrings, wished me happiness and a long life, and sent me away. I was baffled. Just minutes ago, she made me cry, and now she was wishing me well?

That day, I saw two extreme sides of life. In one moment, I was surrounded by love and laughter, and in the next, I was breaking down in frustration. It was the day I realized that life keeps moving — happiness and sadness can exist in the same span of hours. And because of that, I promised myself to live in the moment and cherish the good as it comes.

When I returned to my hostel that evening, I found gifts from my friends waiting for me. As I unwrapped them, I reflected on everything that had happened. That birthday taught me something important—not every moment is perfect, but the ones filled with love always outweigh the ones that bring us down.

Anatomy: The First Encounter with Mortality

Anatomy became the cornerstone of my first-year experience, not just as a subject but as an emotional journey. The first day in the anatomy lab is etched in my memory. The sharp smell of formalin teared up my eyes, burning my throat and nose. The sheer sensory assault was overwhelming, but the emotional weight of what I was about to witness far outweighed it.

I remember standing by the cadaver for the first time, my heart pounding in my chest. The lifeless body lying before us wasn't just a "specimen"; it was a person who had lived, loved, and dreamed. My hands trembled as I held the scalpel, torn between awe and fear. Over time, I grew accustomed to the formalin and the sight of cadavers, but the reverence never faded. Every dissection was a humbling reminder of the trust these individuals had placed in us by donating their bodies for our education.

But the anatomy lab wasn't just a place of learning; it was also a place of frustration and resilience. The head of the department, who also happened to be our hostel warden, made life difficult for us. Her rigid rules and invasive practices—like checking our phones—felt suffocating. She was harsh, anti-feminist, and left little room for understanding. I remember the fear and anger I felt when she tried to impose her authority on every aspect of our lives. Yet, navigating her rules taught me to stand my ground, to assert my boundaries, and to find strength in adversity.

Biochemistry: The Battle of Concepts

If anatomy was emotional, biochemistry was intellectually draining. Understanding metabolic pathways and the endless cycles often felt like trying to decipher an alien language. I remember one night, sitting at my desk, staring at the same diagram of the Krebs cycle for hours, frustration building until I could barely think. I doubted whether I could ever master it.

But then came small victories. Solving a complex question in class or finally understanding a topic I'd struggled with for weeks brought a quiet satisfaction. Biochemistry taught me patience—the ability to push through confusion and self-doubt to find clarity on the other side.

Physiology: The Heartbeat of Understanding

Physiology was where science met life. Learning how the heart beats, how the lungs expand, how the body adapts—it was like uncovering the secrets of existence. But with this knowledge came emotional weight. I remember the lecture on cardiac arrest, vividly imagining a heart stopping, a life ending. It made me realize the fragility of life, even as I marveled at the resilience of the human body.

The practicals were equally engaging. I vividly recall the first time I heard my own heartbeat through a stethoscope. It was surreal, hearing the rhythmic sound that had kept me alive every moment of my life. Physiology wasn't just about reading; it was about experiencing the human body in ways I'd never imagined.

The Need to Belong

While navigating these academic challenges, I also wrestled with the incessant need to make friends. Everyone around me seemed so confident, so sure of themselves, while I felt like an outsider, awkward and unsure. I tried to connect with as many people as possible, hoping to find "my group," the ones who would make this journey feel less daunting. Slowly but surely, I found my circle—people who laughed with me, supported me, and reminded me that I wasn't alone.

The Emotional Weight of This Year

The first year of medical school was an emotional rollercoaster. There were days of exhilaration, like the first time I correctly identified a nerve in the dissection hall or passed a difficult internal exam. There were nights of despair when homesickness hit hard, or when the weight of expectations felt unbearable.

I began the year feeling liberated, as though a weight had been lifted, only to realize there were many more hurdles ahead. But as the year came to a close, I felt stronger, more confident, and ready to face whatever lay ahead.

There were nights I cried myself to sleep, questioning if I had made the right choice. There were mornings where I felt a surge of pride, knowing I was carving my own path. There were moments of loneliness that felt unbearable and moments of laughter with newfound friends that made everything worth it.

Somewhere along the way, I found love, a quiet but comforting presence that made the journey a little less lonely. Their words, soft yet powerful, had a way of dissolving my doubts, and their belief in me was a constant reminder that I was never truly alone. Through it all, my best friends remained my rock. Despite the miles between us, their words of encouragement and endless video calls kept me grounded. I'll never forget how they celebrated my smallest victories and pulled me out of my darkest days, all through the glow of a tiny screen.

Conclusion: A Year That Changed Everything

This year was unlike anything I had ever experienced. It wasn't just about academics—it was about growth, about learning to be alone and being okay with it. It was about facing emotions I never knew I had, about finding strength in solitude, about realizing that I could miss home so much and yet still find moments of happiness here. I can call it a Transformative Year. It taught me resilience, humility and the importance of living in the moment.

If there's one thing this year taught me, it's that **uncertainty doesn't mean failure—it means possibilities**. I may not have had all the answers when I stepped into this journey, but maybe, just maybe, I didn't need them. Maybe I just needed to take it one step at a time and trust that I belonged.

The first year of medical school didn't just teach me about anatomy, biochemistry, or physiology. It taught me about myself. And with the transition to the second year on the horizon, I knew the journey was only just beginning.

THE ABNORMAL AND THE UNKNOWN: THE TALE TRULY BEGINS HERE!

— *Dr. Madhulika Chaudhury, MBBS,*
SVIMS- Sri Padmavathi Medical College for Women, Tirupati, AP, India.

*"I had never expected medicine to be such a lawless, uncertain world.
I wondered if the compulsive naming of parts, diseases, and chemical
reactions— frenulum, otitis, glycolysis— was a mechanism invented by
doctors to defend themselves against a largely unknowable sphere of
knowledge. The profusion of facts obscured a deeper and more significant
problem: the reconciliation between knowledge (certain, fixed, perfect,
concrete) and clinical wisdom
(uncertain, fluid, imperfect, abstract)."*

— Siddhartha Mukherjee,
The Laws of Medicine: Field Notes from an Uncertain Science

2

THE ABNORMAL AND THE UNKNOWN: THE TALE TRULY BEGINS HERE!

— Dr. Madhulika Chaudhury, MBBS,
SVIMS- Sri Padmavathi Medical College for Women, Tirupati, AP, India.

Second year of medical school. The longest. The toughest year alongside final year – well, at least academically. Just as we are settling in, after our new experiences of first year – bam! – Here is a platter of another dose of new!

This is the year when we venture a little beyond all the "normal" that we got to study – we got to study about the diseases – not just in our books but the opportunity to actually see the mysteries of the human body unravel in real life - our clinical rotations to various specialities had begun. A regular three-hour trip to the clinical wards and the out-patient department became a part of our routine. The initial few days were filled with enthusiasm with a hint of anxiety and fear. Properly pressed, wrinkle -free whitecoats whose pockets were laden with the paraphernalia of medicine (and loads of pens because we would inevitably lose one every day to a post-graduate trainee who never bothered to return it!). Stethoscope, knee-hammer, torchlight - you name it and we had it. Yes, we were ready for anything that came our way - at least we believed we did.

Three semesters. Four subjects. Eighteen months. It was long and hard.

Third Semester

The third semester (the first semester of second year) is considered the 'honey-moon period', essentially because there was no exam to be taken for the next one year and because no one in the clinics expected us to know anything so we were never asked much. Blissful six months. Time, which otherwise is a luxury to medical students, seems not to move forward during this semester. It is not long before the guilt of not having to study rigorously starts to pester us to the point when we crave for an exam to prepare for. Paradoxical, but that is how we are wired since our school days.

Slowly and expectedly, our academic life starts getting serious again. Knowingly or unknowingly, we all imbibe the essence of what this year expects of us. Our clinics and long hours of lectures does ultimately, somehow, make us understand what we were supposed to learn in this semester – an understanding of the basics of human disease, a glimpse of medicine in its scientific and artistic form, and vital information that we would be coming back to time-and-again, for the rest of our lives, to make sense of the big picture.

For most of us, the enthusiasm to start with reading the 'standard' textbooks sometimes dwindled down to reading our friends' notes to get through the examinations. But information is information. Truth be told, more often than not, it is what we see in our clinics that saves us to fill in those pages of our answer scripts – a lot of times, subconsciously so.

While our textbooks are filled with tables and columns and classifications and patterns of diseases, the clinics used to tell a different tale of medicine. Not in the scientific essence of medicine, but in the way we would come to the right diagnosis. Dealing with people is no easy task, but for the optimist it is an adventure, for each patient has a story to recount about the disease and their bodies have a tale unfolding in front of you – a tale whose script is now handed over to you.

Fourth Semester

Six months in, one entire set of examinations later, here we were – ready to take on the fourth semester! Now that we were shaken off the torpor of third semester, academics took a serious front in our lives again. With a renewed focus on our academics, a lot of us started planning what we would do after this course ended. So many opportunities, so many possibilities, so much hope. All of us started weighing the pros and cons of the various pathways we could take on – NEET PG, USMLE, PLAB, AMC – I also had an interesting conversation with a batchmate who looked up pursuing PG in Switzerland!

It was a fun and exciting time to prepare ourselves for the future. As days passed by, we understood what was expected of us. We were getting better at history taking and physical examinations of patients. The textbooks started making more sense, even poetic as our clinical understanding increased. We found our friends' circles (and enemies too!). It was lively, a time I would definitely love to re-live knowing how life panned out – I mean this in a good way.

As the rigmarole of our course continued, we all found our outlets to vent out our steam. For some of us, it was the birthdays they organised in the hostel, simple dinners with friends, movie nights and good old 'adda' or 'muchatulu' (general chit-chats which sometimes could turn into heated discussions on politics and philosophy) on various topics in the hostel rooms. I was lucky to be a part of all this having lived as a day-scholar right next to the hostel building. I loved the hostel! It brimmed with positivity – though I realised it was short-lived till the pandemic hit us. *(I say this, because I still remember the time, I had to get some stuff for my friend from her room in the hostel during the pandemic and courier it to her. I will never forget how the hostel was – how empty it was, with their shoes and books and clothes strewn all over the place, evident of how they had to leave the place in a hurry. It was no less than a person alive in the middle of an apocalypse discovering an abandoned building. A place I once knew to be a safe space now seemed so dead and desolate; it was heart-breaking).*

I used to go to the movies with my mum every other week. All Telugu movies. This was something I often flaunted about. I maintained a whole list of movies that I watched that year. It was a beautiful experience to see a culture through the movies they made.

It was also the year when we wished to organise events, at least make an effort to start something – a tradition of sorts for our juniors to follow. This was after we had attended a couple of conferences in other medical colleges that made us realise how important it was to network with other medical students and foster a sense of camaraderie within us. This was not an easy task. It was after a few long discussions with the management (everyone understands how it is to bring about change in an institution, even more so when it is an all-girls college). Finally, we had the wonderful opportunity to organise a dandiya night within the building itself. We transformed the entire four-storey building into a four-floor dance-floor with speakers in every corner. The central clearing and the open space with the music control and small food stalls. It was one of my most memorable nights in that building. We achieved something that night – we set a tradition that continued.

Fifth Semester

My favourite time of this year was during the fifth semester. Almost all of our syllabus was done with. We had gotten into the routine of weekly tests to help us prepare thoroughly for the finals. Clinical rotations became more and more interesting. We had reached a flow state which made room for exciting activities. One of which I fondly remember is Secret Santa during December of 2019. Now, I need you to imagine organising a secret-santa event for a classroom of 150 members! – it was absolutely fun, hilarious and memorable. We even added a small twist to it. The person had to complete a challenge to get the gift from their Secret Santa. I had to sing "Samajavaragamana" and read out a famous monologue by NTR, "Acharyadeva, emantivi, emantivi" on the podium of our classroom to get my gift. It was comical because I struggled with the Telugu words of both the song and the monologue. The gift was a pocket diary, a diary in which I logged in each day's academic record of the pandemic year.

As the year came to an end, our final examinations came closer. It would be two months of absolute turmoil – seven theory papers with four practical exams spread over seven weeks. Even with all the preparation our professors helped us with, it was a scary time. It is during this time that we had to spend night after night studying, sometimes in the library and sometimes in the hostel rooms with our groups to understand concepts better. Everyone had their own way of dealing with exam stress. You learn these behavioural tendencies of your batch-mates quite soon and so learn to give them space or sometimes just be with them – whatever they need.

Once the first exam starts, those weeks pass by in a quick flow. After eighteen months of second year, we just seem to want to get done with it. End, it did. As we wrapped up our final exam for the year in February 2020 (little aware of what was waiting for us the rest of the year), we celebrated happily during the two-day break we got before third year started.

FROM ZOOM CALLS TO EXAM HALLS: THIRD YEAR CHRONICLES!

— *Dr. Darshini Kattula, MBBS,*
SVIMS- Sri Padmavathi Medical College for Women, Tirupati, AP, India.

"Your work is going to fill a large part of your life, and the only way to be truly satisfied is to do what you believe is great work. And the only way to do great work is to love what you do."

— *Steve Jobs.*

3

FROM ZOOM CALLS TO EXAM HALLS: THIRD YEAR CHRONICLES!

— Dr. Darshini Kattula, MBBS,
SVIMS- Sri Padmavathi Medical College for Women, Tirupati, AP, India.

The third year of med school was unlike any other, full of new challenges and personal growth. As the COVID-19 pandemic took over, our world changed, and we had to adapt our medical education in ways we never expected. In this chapter, we'll explore the switch to online classes with their funny moments, the emotional struggles of being isolated, the resilience we built, and the unique experiences of returning to college for post-pandemic exams. These moments shaped us into more adaptable and compassionate future doctors.

In the third year of Med School, we gained efficient clinical exposure by taking turns to examine patients and present cases, building our clinical knowledge. The ensuing discussions engaged the entire team, fostering a collaborative clinical mindset.

"History taking is an art"- this sentence was more pronounced as we started taking the history from patients. Understanding the case, simplifying it, noting down the most important aspects in the case and highlighting the things which point out to a definitive diagnosis was the main aim while presenting cases.

Adapting to a New Reality

My third year began two days after my second year exams were finished in February 2020. We started the third year with all of our energy and enthusiasm. Social and Preventive Medicine (SPM), ENT, and OPHTHALMOLOGY are third-year subjects that have distinct foundations. Since we had already studied the fundamentals in first and second year, it felt important to review the anatomy and physiology of the ears, nose, throat, and eyes as soon as lessons started.

As soon as our classes started, our professors began going over the core concepts. After clinical postings began, all medical students benefited greatly from the opportunity to learn and obtain knowledge in a more visual way. About a week after the start of our third year, on March 18, 2020 - a day etched in my mind, the shocking news of the COVID-19 LOCKDOWN was announced. An emotional roller coaster, whether you view it as a significant vacation or a respite to recharge after two years of MBBS.

All our lives were drastically altered by the COVID-19 pandemic. The first few days felt like an extended vacation. However, during the long days of mental strain, nothing is remembered despite knowing everything. However, self-care and self-motivation made us stronger every day.

Digital Learning and the Return to In-Person Tests

Online classes during the pandemic brought a mix of amusement and monotony. There were moments when someone's camera would unexpectedly turn on, revealing hilarious backgrounds or unexpected family members. We had instances of music playing in the background, and even some classmates caught dozing off, much to the professors' dismay. Despite the occasional boredom, these quirky incidents made the virtual learning experience memorable and kept us all connected in laughter.

The emotional toll of being disconnected from our classmates and traditional classrooms was profound. Medicine, often learned through shared experiences and hands-on collaboration, became a solitary endeavor, making grasping complex concepts more challenging. The lack of face-to-face interactions with peers and mentors left many of us feeling isolated and overwhelmed. However, we persevered, finding creative ways to stay connected and support each other despite the distance.

The last three months of our third year were a whirlwind of clinical postings and exam stress. Returning to college to sit for exams once the

COVID-19 situation was under control felt surreal. Pre-pandemic, our days were filled with hands-on learning, patient interactions, and bustling campus life. But post-COVID, everything was different—the sense of urgency, the heightened precautions, and the underlying tension. Despite the challenges, we adapted, finding new ways to support each other and navigate this transformed environment. The resilience and camaraderie we developed during these times are what made it all worthwhile.

What we See

In the third year of medical school, it is always crucial to connect the topic to the anatomy and physiology of vision that we covered in the first year. Through 3D images and virtual movies of eye anatomy, we can visualise eye structures that are invisible to the human sight. Since we were little children, many of us have found the testing of visual acuity to be an intriguing experience. It was fascinating to visualise the cataract procedures and ophthalmoscopy examinations.

Case studies and case reports were crucial in helping us grasp the material from a foundational to a more advanced level. This year, the patient-based learning approach was the mainstay, but we missed it because of the COVID-19 pandemic. Learning the OPHTHALMOLOGY more efficiently requires memorisation of the structures and the application of imaginary memory. We all watched virtual versions of cataract, Lasik, traumatic eye surgery, and foreign body removal procedures, which increased our interest in theoretical information.

What we Hear

The anatomy of the head and neck, which we studied in our first year, is now a crucial component of this course. Relearning anatomy and physiology in ENT reminded me of my first year. Since the anatomy of the head and neck was difficult to understand, memorising and visualising it was crucial to better understanding the disorders of the ears, nose, and throat. Only these two courses, which are prerequisites for all medical students, allowed for the comprehensive method of assessing a patient's history, evaluating clinical cases, and ultimately arriving at a final diagnosis. It took a lot more work and effort to understand the names of the various muscles, motions, and thorough knowledge of throat illnesses.

We found the ENT online courses to be very helpful. Even though we were unable to see the surgeries in operating rooms and OPDs, we were still able to view all of the procedures and surgeries in videos and recordings. We were introduced to the subject in both theory and clinical practice through daily virtual case presentations and case discussions in the online classes. It is fascinating but tiresome to discuss the topics on an online platform.

What we Explore

Our first year of Medical School, SPM lessons began, and in our second year, our lecturers finished the coursework. SPM was a fascinating subject because it combined medical knowledge with the everyday lives of individuals and communities. In our second year, we used to visit a lot of locations while on SPM posts, including medical camps, sub centres, PHC, CHC, village rural health survey, anganwadis, water purification plants, vaccination centres, and many more.

We all found it fascinating to go on field trips and discover a lot of novel and inventive things. We are always interested in learning new things when we visit many homes in rural and tribal areas to conduct family health-based surveys.

However, because of the pandemic, we were only able to take SPM classes online in the third year, and our entire batch was deprived of the opportunity to experience actual community medicine postings and classes in our galleries. The main focus of the third year is learning biostatistics in community medicine. The primary objective shifted to learning all of the statistics formulas and terminology by heart. Students (the future doctors) are greatly aided by community and field-based medicine in promoting "health for all" and seeking treatment for those who are unable to do so in rural locations.

We learnt from community medicine how important it is to promote the advantages of healthcare for all communities across the nation. Although it was a little exhausting to learn and memorise the schemes, vaccinations, dates, scales, and computations, once one realised how important they were, it became a top priority to finish them while studying the subject. It is truly a lovely feeling to arrive at college with a big smile on your face and a heavy heart, finally, after the lockdown. In order to take our tests, we attended a few clinical lessons, and we passed them with flying colours.

Our third year in medical school was a wild ride filled with events, emotions, learning about the future, and living the LIFE during COVID. All our lives were greatly impacted by our professors, mentors, teachers, family, and friends, who served as a constant source of support and encouragement as they worked towards becoming EFFECTIVE FUTURE DOCTORS.

THE PANDEMIC: A YEAR WE'LL NEVER FORGET

— Dr. Gowrava Vijayalakshmi, MBBS,
SVIMS- Sri Padmavathi Medical College for Women, Tirupati, AP, India.

"What comes easy won't last. What lasts won't come easy."

— *Unknown*

4

THE PANDEMIC: A YEAR WE'LL NEVER FORGET

— Dr. Gowrava Vijayalakshmi, MBBS,
SVIMS- Sri Padmavathi Medical College for Women, Tirupati, AP, India.

The COVID-19 pandemic was an unprecedented event that dramatically impacted our lives, especially as medical students. It brought about significant changes in our routines, experiences, and perspectives. Here, I recount the events and lessons learned during this extraordinary period. The Beginning: A Sudden Shift It all started on December 19, 2020, when a deadly virus emerged from China and spread across the world. At the time, we were having our 2nd year MBBS exams, So we were just hearing about it on social media platforms that the coronavirus was spreading everywhere. We completed our 2nd year MBBS exams, and immediately our 3rd year MBBS classes began. Slowly, cases started increasing in our institute, and some of our students and university staff got infected. Our administration decided to stop offline classes. Suddenly, one evening in 2020, our management passed a circular to vacate the hostel within a day. We were stunned, wondering how it was possible to vacate within 24 hours. North Indian students faced many challenges in traveling back home. While most of us felt happy to get holidays, vacating the hostel with all our luggage was tough. We requested our management to provide a few rooms to store our belongings, and they accepted. We arranged everything and went to our homes.At first, we were happy being at home, but slowly the reality hit us. COVID-19 started spreading to our areas, making it very difficult for our parents to go to work and step outside. They found it challenging to breathe through masks, and many of our parents were diabetics and hypertensive. As medicos, knowing about the risks and complications and the increased risk of infection due to comorbidities, our minds were filled with fear.

Online Classes and New Routines

During our 3ʳᵈ MBBS, classes continued on online platforms. Here's a glimpse of our typical day during those times: Everyone joined the online class with their video off and muted, just for the sake of attendance. No one responded to questions; it was like the professors were shouting in class, but no one cared. We dozed off during classes, chit-chatted on social media, and sometimes, by mistake, our video and audio would turn on, allowing our professors to hear different voices of our family members, which was found to be very funny to others in the class. Proxy attendance was easy, sleeping during classes, chit-chatting with stickers in WhatsApp groups, professors' frustration, taking screenshots without reviewing them, signal issues, online exams, cheating and sending PDFs—

Everything was so funny during online classes. At first, we were excited to go home and enjoy a break from our usual hectic schedules. However, as the days passed and the severity of the pandemic became more apparent, our excitement turned into concern and uncertainty. The unknown situation left us feeling anxious about what the future held.Discovering New Hobbies: Cooking Adventures

One unexpected hobby that emerged during the pandemic was cooking. We had so much time on our hands that we began exploring new recipes and sharing our creations on social media. Even though it was difficult to get groceries, especially in cities, delivery agents played a major role during those tough days. I am really grateful to the delivery boys.

Facing the Hospital Challenges

Our hospital was declared a COVID hospital where testing and treatment for corona patients were done. During that time, our seniors were doing their internship with literally hectic postings, wearing personal protection kits, N95 masks, and face masks, which made it so difficult to breathe. Our doctors, seniors, and hospital staff working in the hospital, going back home to their families with fear in mind about the virus even after precautions. Despite so many efforts, many staff lost their lives. Situations became so serious and tough that most of our families and relatives got affected by the coronavirus. At that time, finding a bed in the hospital was so tough. Patients' saturation was falling, but oxygen cylinder prices were hiking. Oxygen cylinders were not available at all; their prices skyrocketed. Somehow, we found a bed and arranged treatment for our families and relatives. After all the efforts, hearing 'no more' was the worst thing to handle. This was just from our side. Thinking about the patients who don't have any knowledge about the virus and the hospital environment, imagine the situation of patients and attenders wearing masks, roaming all over the hospital for tests, medicines, bills, food, and maintenance of their patients, while they should communicate to other family members at home. After so many efforts from doctors, nurses, technicians, pharmacists, ward boys, patient attenders, management, and watchmen, some patients got out of the risk successfully. Some patients lost their lives. We are very grateful to each and every hospital staff. The fear of the virus was constant as doctors, seniors, and hospital staff worked tirelessly. We witnessed the emotional toll it took on families and patients. The news of our seniors being called for duties was alarming, and the strict rules added to our anxiety.

The Financial Impact on Healthcare

In those days, the cost of all medicines hiked so much that pharma companies made a lot of money. Many people were selling injections of REMDESVIR, tablets of IVERMECTIN, PARACETAMOL, CETEIRIZINE, etc., and oxygen cylinders on the back door without knowing anything about medicines. At that tough time, luckily, we got sanctioned with an oxygen plant by the government, which saved so much money and many lives.

Family Time and Adjustments

Despite all the challenges, we got to spend quality time with our families, something we rarely had before. We bonded over cooking, shared stories, scrolled through Instagram, and found comfort in each other's presence. This period allowed us to enjoy the simple joys of life and appreciate our loved ones more. However, going back to college after such a long break was difficult, as everything felt new and we realized how much we had missed.

The Second Wave: A Tougher Battle

Just when we thought things were returning to normal, the second wave of COVID-19 hit, affecting more people, especially in rural areas. We took COVISHIELD and COVAXIN vaccine shots, and the government took precautions by announcing lockdowns and supplying vaccines. Despite these efforts, the second wave was more severe, and we lost many close people. The situations during the second wave were worse than the first, and it tested our resilience once again.

Lessons Learned and Moving Forward

Being at home during the pandemic, we learned so many things. We saw many sufferings related to both physical, mental, and professional problems, and we fought them with a very strong mindset. Meanwhile, we learned household work and enjoyed every moment with family. We are very,

very thankful to all management and each and every hospital staff. Finally, the pandemic period left us with a great bag of mixed emotions, and COVID-19 left the world on May 5th, 2023. We will never forget that year in our lives. It taught us many lessons and shaped our perspectives. Some news broke our hearts, while some gave us courage and calm. We lived to see everything that followed and would probably tell our kids that there was a pandemic when we were in med school and we survived it. The pandemic tested our resilience and adaptability in ways we never imagined. It taught us to face uncertainties with courage, to find strength in our support systems, and to adapt to new circumstances. These lessons will stay with us as we move forward in our medical careers and beyond.

BRIDGING THEORY AND PRACTISE: EMBRACING CHANGE IN CLINICAL TRAINING

— Dr. Arpitha Sirichandana Baggu, MBBS,

SVIMS- Sri Padmavathi Medical College for Women, Tirupati, AP, India.

"The secret to a long and happy life is finding your ikigai — the intersection of what you love, what you're good at, what the world needs, and what you can be paid for."

— Hector Garcia and Francesc Miralles,
Ikigai: The Japanese Secret to a Long and Happy Life.

5

BRIDGING THEORY AND PRACTISE: EMBRACING CHANGE IN CLINICAL TRAINING

— Dr. Arpitha Sirichandana Baggu, MBBS,
SVIMS- Sri Padmavathi Medical College for Women, Tirupati, AP, India.

Leap of Transition

The whole third year went by in the blink of an eye due to COVID leaving us with the final and one of the toughest years of our medical school. This is the year when there has been a huge transition from non-clinical to clinical in terms of knowledge and understanding. It is a major preparation for us to learn how to face patients in real-life settings.

Navigation of The Patient Care

Our professors' lectures in medicine, surgery, obstetrics, and gynecology involve beautiful and concise in-depth teaching from anatomy to the clinical aspect of an organ or the condition. However, just when we enter the clinics to apply the same knowledge taught to us in a four-walled classroom, we enter into a state of tizzy wondering if we're doing it right or if our approach is incorrect. And why is that? One of the things I have slowly learned from my clinical exposure is that all patients don't come with the typical presentation mentioned in the textbooks and that has been taught to us. They need not have all the symptoms mentioned for us to diagnose them with a particular condition. The clinical scenario varies for each patient and it is normal. It is a lifelong learning process that we need to inculcate daily in our clinical experience and history-taking of our patients. With time, we can master it beautifully.

We've all been taught to take history with a set of questions or an algorithm to follow while talking to patients and ruling out certain conditions based on the proforma provided by our seniors and professors. However, they do not provide an idea of how to communicate with the patients effectively. Little did we know that it is one of the most important skills one should have, be it a medical student or a professional. The rapport and trust developed between the patient and the doctor help in getting accurate information required for the diagnosis. There might be a few times when the patient wouldn't be able to answer a few personal questions if we are not able to communicate effectively. Effective communication is the key to understanding a patient way beyond the signs and symptoms to get a whole picture and socio-economic situation of the patient for further affordable and effective treatment plans. One of the cases that I came across at the beginning of my final year was a 63-year-old woman with long-standing diabetes mellitus presented with a severe diabetic foot ulcer, her only remaining limb after amputation of her other foot years earlier. The emotional toll was evident, as she struggled with the thought of losing mobility once again. The emotional and physical challenges she faced served as a reminder diabetes can have on a patient's life. Her journey highlighted the importance of not just clinical care, but compassionate support in managing chronic illness. Many other cases made me realize the application of knowledge and being empathetic towards the patient and their family are equally important.

Examination Skills

The next thing that I would like to talk about is the skills of examining patients. We all might have doubted at least once in our medical school years from histology slides to hearing heart sounds, korotkoff sounds, and the list goes on in each subject wondering if we are watching the exact cells in a slide, hearing the correct sounds, placing the stethoscope in the right position, and performing the lab procedures precisely or not. This continues in the second and third years too, and finally, a peak of self-doubt is attained in the final year of medical school. Though we are taught to examine different organs and systems at their anatomical landmarks, the application of the same requires more practice, which gets better with time. It is ok to feel out of place initially as it is entirely new for us to figure out the differences and understand every aspect of the examination. Once we figure it out, then the beauty of history-taking and examination is phenomenal.

Diagnostic Challenges

WHAT'S NEXT??? After completing the first two steps, we now face lab reports, X-rays, and other scans, leaving me wondering if I could ever pull off being a good doctor. I am still in the process of learning it, though, and the practice of interpreting it correctly develops with time. Interpretation of the lab reports and x-rays supplements the findings in history and clinical examination. So, we also need to learn to correlate our findings with the patient's symptoms. It is so important for us to learn and improve our critical thinking toward a correct diagnosis because a small change in interpretation can lead us to a different diagnosis.

Overcoming Anxiety Through Case Presentation

We then write a nice case to present with everything asked and examined. Now comes the task of presenting your case findings to your attending and professor. It might be exciting for some and cause anxiety and tension for other students. But all this is a starting step for overcoming our fear and anxiety to unlock greater knowledge and critical thinking skills. Our attendings and professors teach us and make us think in a multidisciplinary approach, which can improve our diagnosing ability, decision-making, and critical thinking skills.

Gradual Growth

These baby steps which we take each year by interacting with each patient and applying our theoretical knowledge gradually in the clinical setting will help us become an efficient doctor. ALL THIS SERIOUS TALK ASIDE, WHAT YOU HAVE TO DO IS VERY SIMPLE...JUST TALK TO THE PATIENTS WHENEVER YOU CAN!!!! I wish I had done this way early. Do not ever hesitate to speak to your patients. It is fine if you do not know anything about the condition of the patient, but you can learn from that situation, go back home, and then you can recall whatever you have communicated with them. The least we can do is give moral support and show empathy. One of the physicians under whom I have observed advised me that we should not do things for the sake of doing them. We should try being compassionate in interacting with every patient and their family too.

DOCTOR IN THE MAKING: MY INTERNSHIP JOURNEY

— *Dr. Vijetha Reddy Katta, MBBS,*
SVIMS- Sri Padmavathi Medical College for Women, Tirupati, AP, India.

"Medicine is a science of uncertainty and an art of probability."

— William Osler

6

DOCTOR IN THE MAKING: MY INTERNSHIP JOURNEY

— *Dr. Vijetha Reddy Katta, MBBS,*
SVIMS- Sri Padmavathi Medical College for Women, Tirupati, AP, India.

Every year of medical school was an incredible journey. After completing my final year, with immense joy and anticipation, I stepped into my internship. Internship is undoubtedly the most exhilarating year of the entire medical curriculum. This stage is where the knowledge we have gained meets real-world application, and it is during this time that a medical student truly transforms into a doctor.

The First Lesson

My very first day as an intern began with a night shift in the Department of Emergency Medicine. Hoping to stay alert, I packed my bag with snacks, fruits, and a flask of hot milk. But by the time my duty ended, I hadn't even opened them—it was that busy. Breaks were a luxury, and every minute was consumed by the fast-paced chaos of the ER.

As interns, we were responsible for triage, attending to patients as they arrived, assessing cases, and informing the postgraduate residents, who would then decide on admissions. At times, ambulances would line up outside, reminding me of scenes from my favorite series, Grey's Anatomy. Initially, the adrenaline rush was exciting, but over time, I realized how exhausting and demanding the job truly was. Thankfully, emergency duties were divided into three shifts, allowing us to get adequate rest afterward.

Around the fourth or fifth day of my internship, I had a nerve-wracking experience—I accidentally pricked my hand with a needle right after administering an injection to a patient. Worse still, I wasn't even wearing gloves. I noticed a small amount of blood at the site of the prick and immediately reported it to my seniors. They warned me about the risk of transmissible diseases, and after some discussion, we decided to run tests on the patient. He was a middle-aged man with a history of chronic alcoholism, admitted with abdominal pain. However, when I went to find him, he had absconded. I searched everywhere, only to be told by staff that this was a common occurrence. I was terrified and almost broke into tears. My seniors reassured me, advising me to monitor myself for symptoms and take precautionary tests if needed. Thankfully, everything turned out fine, but that moment stayed with me. It was a harsh lesson in the importance of precaution and self-protection in this field.

The Foundation of Medicine

Medicine postings were instrumental in shaping clinical knowledge. It was here that I conducted my first independent outpatient (OP) session. Typically, interns assist PGs and attendings in OP, but one day, I was left to manage it alone when my seniors were called for a sudden meeting. Though initially nervous, I handled it well and that experience significantly boosted my confidence and cleared self-doubts—true milestones.

In the wards, where patients were admitted for extended periods, we monitored vitals, managed medications, and interacted with them daily. This naturally led to forming bonds with patients, making their recovery and gratitude deeply fulfilling. There's an indescribable joy in seeing a patient express heartfelt thanks upon discharge—it makes all the hard work feel truly worthwhile.

Once a woman was admitted in critical condition with severe pneumonia caused by a bacterial infection. She had been experiencing high fever, difficulty breathing, and extreme weakness for several days. Upon arrival, her oxygen levels were dangerously low, and despite immediate oxygen support, her condition worsened, necessitating ventilatory support. Outside the ICU, I saw her two young children waiting with their father, a sight that deeply saddened me. The following days were a relentless battle for her survival, with fluctuating vitals and moments of uncertainty. Yet, no one gave up. Through meticulous monitoring, medication adjustments, and dedicated efforts from our senior doctors, she slowly began to improve.

After 15 days, her oxygen levels stabilized, and she was successfully weaned off the ventilator. As she regained consciousness and met her children, tears streamed down her face.

Throughout her recovery, I had been involved in her care, though I wasn't sure if she remembered me or the events that had unfolded. However, before leaving, she smiled with deep gratitude and said, "You all gave me my life back. " That was a heartwarming moment and made me realize the responsibility we carry. There is no greater fulfillment than knowing we played a role in saving a life.

However, not all experiences were uplifting. One of the heartbreaking experiences was the case of a young boy admitted with severe vomiting, diarrhea, and fever. He mentioned having eaten breakfast at a roadside stall before falling ill. At the time of admission, he was conscious and oriented. My friend and I had even shared a lighthearted conversation with him—he spoke about his education, hobbies, and upcoming exams, expressing his eagerness to recover and resume studying.

Unfortunately, his condition deteriorated rapidly. He was severely dehydrated upon arrival, progressing into shock. That night, even after returning to my room, I couldn't stop thinking about him. The next morning, I hurried to his bedside, hoping for signs of improvement, but I learned that he had passed away. He had gone into septic shock, leading to multi-organ failure. I was devastated—just a plate of roadside food had cost this young boy his life, though there was a delay in his presentation to the hospital. The incident left me deeply shaken. It made me realize how unpredictable life is—we never know what will happen next.

The Hospital Ecosystem

Before my internship, I often wondered how a hospital functioned seamlessly. It was during this year that I found the answer. As students, our interactions had been limited to classmates, professors, and patients. But in the real world, we collaborate with an entire ecosystem—attendings, PGs, nurses, ward boys, paramedics, technicians, patients and their attendees, and more. Every skill we acquired came from these individuals. In fact, it was a staff nurse who taught me how to insert an IV cannula. In emergencies, operating theatres, ward management, and various other hospital functions, success is not solely dependent on individual skill but rather on teamwork and collaboration. Even in the most challenging situations, effective coordination enhances efficiency and makes complex tasks more manageable.

Looking up to my senior doctors is truly inspiring—the depth of their knowledge, their unwavering composure, and the wisdom they embody. They remain calm under immense pressure, never panicking even in the most critical situations, skillfully reviving patients on the brink of life. Witnessing their expertise makes the aspiration to become like them feel almost dreamlike. Their dedication and patience have driven me to practice harder and never give up. One day, we aspire to stand in their place, becoming the ones others look up to.

Surgery postings were far from easy. Sleepless nights, chaotic schedules, and demanding tasks defined this phase. From writing case sheets, dressing wounds, collecting and submitting samples, retrieving lab results, escorting patients to scans, and more, every moment was packed. I vividly remember waiting at the blood bank for three hours at 2 AM.

During an emergency laparotomy for a patient with suspected abdominal perforation, the entire surgical team faced an unexpected challenge. Despite thorough exploration, the perforation site remained elusive. The presence of extensive adhesions and bowel distension further complicated the identification process, requiring meticulous examination of each section from the stomach to the intestines. As the procedure extended, it became both physically and mentally demanding. My fellow interns and I were nearly exhausted, as the surgery had already lasted six hours. Finally, after an exhaustive and precise search, the perforation was located in the distal ileum. Without delay, the team proceeded with repair and closure, as prolonging the procedure further significantly increases the risk of complications such as infection and sepsis. This experience was one of the most challenging surgical procedures I encountered.

Despite the exhaustion, assisting in the operating theatre (OT) and learning suturing techniques provided a sense of excitement. The clinical exposure gained during this period was invaluable, offering practical experience before stepping fully into our careers. And amidst all the hard work, there was a small yet fulfilling reward—I received my first-ever stipend. Though minimal, it was my first hard-earned money, and that feeling was truly special.

On a personal note, I love dressing up, wearing accessories, and indulging in makeup. Yet, despite my usual penchant for glam, I found myself embracing my scrubs with pride. There's something about scrubs that instills a sense of identity and belonging in every medico.

Beyond The Hospital

Internship is a challenging phase with an intense workload and prolonged duty hours. The emotional strain inevitably becomes a part of daily life. Amidst these demands, maintaining mental well-being is crucial and should not be overlooked. Engaging in open conversations with colleagues, sharing struggles, and drawing insights from their previous posting experiences can provide valuable support and perspective.

At times, facing criticism or harsh remarks can be disheartening, making it difficult to stay focused. However, rather than internalizing negativity, it is essential to remind ourselves why we chose this profession and view challenges as learning opportunities rather than unnecessary stressors. Developing the ability to remain composed under pressure is a fundamental skill in medicine. Staying positive is key to navigating this journey successfully. Additionally, amidst the relentless schedule, personal time often becomes a rarity. However, setting aside moments for ourselves after shifts is essential for maintaining emotional balance. Engaging in activities that bring joy, spending time with loved ones, and staying connected with family serve as vital sources of mental relaxation and rejuvenation.

The Doctors' cafeteria was our favorite retreat during breaks—a space where everyone gathered to grab a quick bite and unwind. After long, tiring shifts, returning to the hostel and hanging out with my friends was the best part. The late-night conversations, loud laughter, gossip sessions, venting about duties and sharing our experiences gave us the energy to keep going.

The End Of An Era

As our internship neared its end, we organized a series of fests, making the most of our remaining time together. We danced our hearts out, played games, and celebrated every moment. However, beneath all the excitement was the bittersweet realization that this chapter was coming to an end.

From the moment we first stepped into the hospital—filled with excitement, nervousness, and the fear of making mistakes—to emerging as confident, independent doctors, we have undergone immense growth. Internship was not merely about managing medical cases; it was about the people who made the journey truly special—the new people we met and made memories with, the doctors who mentored, the hospital staff who supported, and the fellow interns who shared this transformative experience.

Graduation day was an overwhelming mix of emotions. I felt some sense of pride for having completed this incredible journey. Of course, the internship had its share of ups and downs—friendships, celebrations, conflicts over rosters and duty hours—but, looking back, I don't think any of my mates hold grudges.

Every intern's journey is unique, but what remains common is the unforgettable experiences and the memories we made.

LIFE AFTER GRADUATION: WHEN THE FUTURE FEELS OVERWHELMING AND THE PAST FEELS SAFE

— *Dr. P Sri Sai Githa, MBBS,*
SVIMS- Sri Padmavathi Medical College for Women, Tirupati, AP, India.

"We must accept finite disappointment, but never lose infinite hope."

— Martin Luther King Jr.

7

LIFE AFTER GRADUATION: WHEN THE FUTURE FEELS OVERWHELMING AND THE PAST FEELS SAFE

— Dr. P Sri Sai Githa, MBBS,
SVIMS- Sri Padmavathi Medical College for Women, Tirupati, AP, India.

The urge to constantly live in the future—hasn't it always been that way for most of us? In school, we couldn't wait to get into college. Once in college, we yearned for the so-called freedom of the working world. This pattern has been a recurring theme in my life. During my final year of MBBS, I eagerly anticipated the start of my internship, imagining it to be a phase of endless excitement and freedom.

But guess what? When the "FUN" internship finally began, and I stepped into the real medical world, I found myself longing for the simpler days of being a student. Back then, I could study at my own pace, skip classes guilt-free, and indulge in the occasional extra hour of sleep. In contrast, the internship was a whirlwind of responsibilities—duty and patients always came first. Skipping duty for sleep was unthinkable. Often, you had to set aside your personal life entirely, focusing solely on the hospital and your room. Of course, there were a few postings where you could unwind, but those moments were fleeting.

Soon enough, I began wishing for the internship to end so I could dive into the "REAL" world. But life only gets truly real once you graduate. Now, I'd give anything to go back and relive the internship days! This cycle of yearning for the past or anticipating the future has made me realize a crucial lesson: no matter where we are in life, we often fail to live in the present. Instead, we spend our time reminiscing about the past or chasing an idealized future.

Embracing the Present

The key lesson I've learned is to live in the present. Embrace the now. Make mistakes without fearing them too much, learn from those mistakes, and savor every moment consciously.

Of course, there's immense pressure in this phase of life—the pressure to earn, to settle down quickly, to choose the right branch or institution, and to make decisions your future self won't regret. A thousand questions cloud your mind: Should I take a gap year? Should I work and study simultaneously? Am I on the right path? What is everyone else doing? Add to this the ever-looming parental expectations and that one engineering friend who's already earning lakhs and posting glamorous international trip photos. And here we are, facing an ocean of uncertainty about what the future holds.

But let's take a step back and acknowledge something important: we chose a path that is long and arduous, yet deeply rewarding. There are countless people who would trade places with us in a heartbeat. We've endured so much—academically, mentally, and physically—to reach where we are today. Let's take a moment to appreciate that and cherish the present.

Post-internship is a crucial period, one that requires us to be vigilant and make mindful decisions about our future.

Exploring the Pathways After MBBS

Pursuing Post Graduate studies in INDIA

The most common and classic route is pursuing postgraduate studies (MD/MS) or a diploma (DNB) in a specialty of your choice within India by clearing exams like NEET PG and INICET. You can attempt these exams during your internship period after obtaining a provisional certificate from your college.

- NEET PG is conducted once a year and is the gateway to state government and private postgraduate colleges.
- INICET, held twice a year, offers admission to prestigious central institutes such as AIIMS, PGI, and JIPMER.

Many aspirants opt to take a gap year to prepare for these highly competitive exams. As for resources, Marrow, Prepladder, Bhatia, Cerebellum etc are invaluable for preparation. However, remember the golden rule: "One size does not fit all." Find what works for you and seek guidance from seniors and mentors who have walked this path before you.

MD (Doctor of Medicine)

The MD program offers a wide range of specializations, broadly categorized into clinical and non-clinical branches:

Non-Clinical branches are Anatomy, Physiology, Biochemistry, Pathology, Pharmacology, Microbiology, Preventive Medicine, and Forensic Medicine.

Clinical branches are General Medicine, Pediatrics, Dermatology, Psychiatry, Tuberculosis & Chest Diseases, Anesthesia, Radiodiagnosis, and Radiotherapy.

MS (Master of Surgery)

The MS program focuses on surgical fields, including General Surgery, Orthopedics, Obstetrics and Gynecology, Otorhinolaryngology (ENT), and Ophthalmology.

DNB (Diploma in National Board)

The DNB is a three-year postgraduate program offered by the National Board of Examinations (NBE). Recognized by the National Medical Commission (NMC), this qualification is equivalent to MD/MS degrees. The course is primarily conducted in private hospitals or institutes that meet NMC's standards. Additionally, DNB candidates receive a monthly stipend throughout their program, making it an attractive option for many.

Super Speciality Programs

Certain central and private institutions offer direct six-year super speciality programs post-MBBS through INICET and NEET PG.

D.M (Doctorate of Medicine)

Specializations include Cardiology, Gastroenterology, Endocrinology, Oncology, Hematology, Neurology, and Nephrology.

M.Ch (Magister Chirurgiae)

Specializations include Cardiothoracic Surgery, Oncosurgery, Plastic Surgery, Gastrointestinal Surgery, Hepatobiliary Surgery, Neurosurgery, Pediatric Surgery, and Urology.

Government Jobs

Shall we now explore the most certain way to secure stability and perhaps even win the admiration of your future partner? Let's talk about government jobs.

Medical Officer Roles

MBBS graduates can work as medical officers in both government and private institutions. Recruitment typically occurs through competitive examinations or open job advertisements. The former is common for government roles, while the latter applies to private institutions.

Union Public Service Commission (UPSC)

The UPSC conducts the Combined Medical Services (CMS) examination annually to recruit medical professionals for various government institutions. Positions include:
- Junior Scale Posts in Central Health Services
- Assistant Divisional Medical Officer in the Railways
- General Duty Medical Officer in Municipal Councils

Teaching Roles

Graduates can also join medical colleges as tutors in their chosen specialty, with recruitment often occurring through job advertisements.

Armed Forces Medical Services (AFMS)

For those drawn to serving in the military, navy, or air force, the Armed Forces Medical Services (AFMS) offers a promising career. Doctors commissioned in the Indian Army join as Captains in the Army Medical Corps. Promotions are awarded at regular intervals, ensuring career growth.

Postgraduate Opportunities Abroad

One of the most popular and increasingly pursued options is residency or postgraduate education outside India. The following exams pave the way for such opportunities:

- USMLE (United States Medical Licensing Examination) for the U.S.
- PLAB (Professional and Linguistic Assessments Board) for the U.K.
- AMC (Australian Medical Council) exams for Australia
- And several other country-specific exams.

Each pathway has its unique set of requirements and advantages, but all provide access to advanced training, global exposure, and rewarding career opportunities.

__"For those exploring paths beyond NEET PG, including exams like USMLE, PLAB, AMC, DHA, or NCMZ, a concise guide awaits at the end of the book to help you navigate these options."__

The Journey from Passion to Burnout

Most of us entered medical school at the tender age of 18 or 20, brimming with ambition and a deep-seated passion for the profession. Back then, many of us didn't fully grasp what we were signing up for, but we embarked on this path with starry eyes and a hopeful heart.

Fast forward 5.5 years—after countless exams, sleepless nights, grueling schedules, and relentless pressure—some of us may find that the initial spark has dimmed. The love for medicine that once drove us may feel like a distant memory, buried under the weight of burnout and fatigue. You might even find yourself thinking, "Haven't I taken enough exams already? I can't bear the thought of another one."

If this resonates with you, trust me—you're not alone. And here's the good news: Your career doesn't end here.

Alternative Career Paths for MBBS Graduates

If clinical or preclinical roles aren't appealing, several alternative career pathways can align with your interests:

Hospital Management and Administration (MHA/MBA):

Institutions offer three-year postgraduate degrees in hospital management and administration (MHA/MBA). With the rapid growth of private hospitals and healthcare institutions, there is a rising demand for MBBS graduates in medical administration. This field is ideal for those inclined toward administration, hospitality, or entrepreneurship.

For those aiming higher, an MBA from prestigious institutions like the IIMs can be pursued by clearing the CAT examination.

Medical writing involves creating scientific content for regulatory, educational, or promotional purposes in healthcare. Key types include regulatory writing (clinical reports), scientific writing (research papers), and content writing (blogs, patient education). Industries employing medical writers include pharmaceutical companies, CROs, medical communication agencies, and healthcare startups. Skills required include strong medical knowledge, technical writing proficiency, and familiarity with guidelines (e.g., ICH-GCP, FDA). Career progression ranges from junior medical writer to senior roles like team lead or freelance consultant. Demand is driven by the growth of the global healthcare industry and clinical trial documentation needs. Emerging opportunities exist in digital health content, including apps and telemedicine. Remote and freelance roles make it a flexible career choice with diverse opportunities. It is a rewarding field for those with a passion for science, communication, and writing.

Content creation after MBBS offers diverse opportunities, combining medical expertise with creative communication. Graduates can explore roles in medical writing, health blogging, health journalism, patient education, and creating online courses or video content for platforms like YouTube or social media. Industries such as digital health startups, pharmaceutical companies, and media outlets actively hire medical content creators. Essential skills include simplifying complex medical concepts, writing, video editing, and familiarity with SEO and digital tools. This career offers flexibility, remote work options, and entrepreneurial ventures like freelancing or personal branding. There is a high demand for credible, expert-backed health content, and earnings range from ₹3–6 LPA in India for beginners, with significant growth potential for experienced creators.

Pursuing a career in research and academia after MBBS offers a fulfilling path for those passionate about medical advancements, education, and shaping healthcare policies. Many opt for a PhD in medical sciences or specialize in research fields like pharmacology, microbiology, or epidemiology, while others pursue an MD/MS before transitioning into academia. Teaching positions in medical colleges, public health institutions, and curriculum development are common academic roles. Research opportunities exist in clinical trials, biomedical sciences, and health policy, often through fellowships for postdoctoral programs. Renowned institutions like AIIMS, PGIMER, ICMR, and global universities provide excellent platforms for research. Government bodies such as ICMR, WHO, and NIH also offer medical research roles. Additionally, careers in pharmaceutical research, biotech, and medical writing are viable options. Success in this field requires expertise in research methodologies, data analysis, scientific publishing, and grant writing. Building strong academic networks and collaborating on impactful projects further enhance career prospects.

The medical field is vast and diverse, offering endless opportunities for growth, fulfillment, and rediscovery. Sometimes, all it takes is stepping back, reevaluating your priorities, and exploring alternative pathways that align with your current aspirations and mindset.

Burnout is not a sign of failure; it's a signal to pause, reassess, and chart a course that reignites your purpose. Your journey in medicine doesn't have to follow a single, rigid trajectory—it's your path to define.

HEALING THE HEALERS: MENTAL HEALTH AND MORE

— Dr. Prashasti Sharma, MBBS,
SVIMS- Sri Padmavathi Medical College for Women, Tirupati, AP, India.

"There are wounds that never show on the body that are deeper and more hurtful than anything that bleeds."

— Laurell K. Hamilton

8

HEALING THE HEALERS: MENTAL HEALTH AND MORE

— Dr. Prashasti Sharma, MBBS,
SVIMS- Sri Padmavathi Medical College for Women, Tirupati, AP, India.

The Overhyped Beginning

First day of medical school you walk in thrilled at having achieved the -overhyped "medical student" status. Reality however, seldom matches the expectations. Suddenly you find yourself in uncharted territory. From being the golden child, the overachiever, the all-rounder in high school, you're now just one among many highly talented individuals. This marks the birth of toxic competitiveness and a persistent feeling of inadequacy.

Being the smartest person in the room is no longer your reality, leading to an identity crisis. Who am I without my perfect grades?

Most of us were either bullied about being 'nerds' or praised for our academic achievements to the point where love started feeling conditional and being "nerdy" became our identity. As a result academic validation was tied to love and self worth. Falling short academically felt like a betrayal to everyone who "believed " in us. This sudden identity shift is drastic and students find themselves lost and unable to cope. It is no wonder that the infamous Imposter Syndrome runs rampant in medical schools.

In my experience, most people who land in this profession find some of the following points relatable - people with buckets of empathy looking to heal a part of themselves by healing others, kids who chase academic validation to feel worthy of love, true intellectuals with a thirst for knowledge and finally those who got pressured into it by family with no clear way forward.

First year: Cadavers and Conditioning

First year of medical school introduces you to anatomy and, of course, cadavers. Dealing with death became the new norm early on. Strict rules for attendance and hearing words like "why did you take a sick day off? Are you more unwell than the patients?" were common during our training. Was it tough love? Or just brutal? This conditioning early on affected our long term behaviours such as an inability to take breaks or guilt when prioritizing basic self care. A place that doesn't hold space for physical health issues obviously holds none for mental health.

Till date, most of us find it unthinkable to call work and have the privilege to give time to ourselves on days when we truly need it. Days when you just want to stay in bed and regulate your nervous system, or get a couple more hours of sleep, or read the book that's been on your list for months, or catch up with your best friend or just sit in comforting silence.

Never-ending series of exams and publicly shaming those who did not perform well is also something that isn't unheard of. When do we begin acknowledging the dire human need to pause and take a breath? To relax and to enjoy life. Humans are inherently social creatures meant to connect with nature and each other but we forget to spend time with our loved ones in this never-ending race fuelled by ambition. Medical students often find themselves missing important family events, leading to an alienation to the concept of having a social and personal life.

What does true happiness mean to you? For me it means being kind to myself and loving every version of who I am at every stage of life. Spending time with my loved ones and appreciating the little things in life. It is watching sunsets with a cup of coffee in hand, receiving a warm hug on a cold day, or not waking up with a PACKED to do list. The privilege of living a slow life is what I would like to give myself.

Chasing an Empty Ideal

What good are countless degrees if you are intrinsically unhappy and perpetually at the brink of a breakdown? When I look around and see doctors, I usually come across deeply burnt-out people who feel inadequate no matter how much they push themselves. We chase degrees, titles and accolades hoping they'll help fill the emptiness within. But they never do, leaving us trapped in a never-ending cycle of seeking external validation for a change that can only come from within. When will we learn that we cannot help others if we are not truly there for ourselves. Doctors are often on the front lines of witnessing suffering and death, which can lead to vicarious trauma, depression, or anxiety. On top of this, the stigma surrounding mental health in the medical profession itself can prevent doctors from seeking help. There's a cultural expectation that doctors need to be tough, unshakable, and always " on the go". But this can perpetuate a cycle where their own mental health needs are neglected, which affects their ability to connect with and care for their patients.

For doctors, emotional unavailability might not be a reflection of a lack of empathy or compassion, but rather a defense mechanism to protect themselves from burnout. The emotional toll of constantly being exposed to illness, trauma, and suffering can leave healthcare providers feeling numb or detached, a survival instinct in an environment where there is often not enough time or resources to truly connect with patients.

For patients, this emotional unavailability can be disheartening and frustrating. When people are facing health challenges, they often need not just physical treatment but emotional support, empathy, and a sense of being heard. If they feel ignored or dismissed, it can exacerbate feelings of anxiety, isolation, and hopelessness.

The Burnout Epidemic

I believe society is self serving, that it praises doctors and places them on a pedestal only to expect endless sacrifice from their side. Congratulations come hand in hand with demands for free treatment alongside a serving of "doctors are money minded" in case you refuse. The guilt that comes with wanting to think about yourself is immense and even seems immoral. It caters to the core people pleasing and self abandonment wounds and makes you push yourself even more.

Understanding that our profession is only a part of our identity is the need of the hour. Asking questions like who am I without the doctor title? What are my beliefs? What do I enjoy? What are my hobbies? What does my ideal life look like without considering the role of external expectations? Happiness is the ultimate goal despite what society brainwashed us to believe. What is true happiness for you? Is the one question I'd implore you to ask yourself.

Unexpressed Emotions - Silent Threat?

Mental health struggles in a field where overworking and self sacrifice is glorified to an inhumane extent, are not surprising and in fact rampant. Working long shifts that run into days, dealing with the pain of patients and their families is something you go through on a daily basis. Experiencing an emotional rollercoaster every time you lose or save a patient in a system that doesn't truly teach students how to cope is how we have ended up with this being one of the professions with the worst mental health statistics.

Each one of us can recall the exact moment when we lost our first patient. How it felt to see their health get better but then suddenly reality takes a turn and you find yourself heart broken, trying to console their family and at a loss of words. With no time to process the kind of impact it's having on you, you're expected to get back to work immediately and get to the next patient. So you put on your smile and brave forwards but you never forget their faces. Days turn into years and patients turn into cases. Doctors get inept at dealing with pain and death after mastering the art of emotional suppression.

As Sigmond Freud rightly said "Unexpressed emotions will never die. They are buried alive and will come forth later in uglier ways". Aka the emergence of a multitude of mental health illnesses that not only affects doctors and their families but also hampers their work efficiency as empathy, sadness and pain are no longer welcome emotions at their place of work.

Understanding that life is more than just academics, that life can exist outside the hospital is something many healthcare workers find difficult to understand. Most doctors I know struggle with immense guilt and shame if they take time off or do something for themselves instead of devoting all their time and energy in climbing up the ladder. It's a never ending rat race and people forget to stop and breath. People forget to be proud of the versions of themselves they are in the present and keep chasing a new goal in the distant future without allowing themselves to enjoy the journey.

Dealing with failure is something that society forgets to teach children. So exams and degrees start feeling like a do or die situation. Exam season anxiety doesn't spare any medical student no matter how hard they push themselves throughout the years. Surviving on hardly any sleep, binging on coffee and pushing each other is how we all sailed through 5.5 years of training.

It's a well known fact that the human brain functions to only a fraction of it's capacity when deprived of sleep. Studies have shown that going too long without sleep can impair your ability to function the same way as drinking too much alcohol. Being awake for at least 18 hours is the same as someone having an alcohol blood content of 0.05% .

It baffles me how in spite of this healthcare workers have shifts spanning days. It is the unsaid obvious that this can be extremely unhealthy and it goes against the physiological needs of the human body, why then do we as medical professionals with ample amounts of knowledge regarding the same fail to see the irony? Are we as a community waging a silent war against our physical and mental selves by conforming to the system? Is this just a socially acceptable form of self harm? Would we want someone who is under the influence of alcohol to diagnose, treat or operate on us or our loved ones? If not then how can we practice something that could actually put so many lives at risk just because we forget to let ourselves REST.

Destigmatizing Mental Health in Medicine

I've heard people including doctors make jokes at the expense of psychiatric patients, which is not only highly insensitive but also unprofessional and disheartening. If educated individuals, specially doctors who are involved in the care and treatment of such patients do not understand the importance of mental health and work towards destigmatising it, what can we expect from the general population?

According to a 2021 study, 40% of physicians surveyed believed that other doctors would view them as less competent if they had a history of depression or anxiety.

Individuals who hold judgement against people suffering from something that is extremely scary and very real will definitely never be able to ask for or accept help if they ever happen to be in a situation where they need it. Unlearning the beliefs we picked up while growing up, educating ourselves and our close ones would make a huge impact in ensuring our loved ones are safe not just physically but also mentally.

The Transformative Power of Therapy

Incorporating mental health into academic curriculum, destigmatising it and ending glamorisation of overworked health care workers is the need of the hour not just for the well being of health care professionals but also for patients in their care. As is widely said - You CANNOT pour from an empty cup.

This is the point where the crucial role of taking therapy comes in. The importance of ensuring therapy is affordable and accessible to all health care professionals could help us avoid losing more precious lives to self harm. Inculcating the importance of mental health from a young age and ensuring that people understand it isn't just for the "crazy" but to help us understand our- selves better, to heal and to nurture. Being self-aware, taking up space for our physical and emotional needs and talking to a professional to help deal with coping strategies that helped us survive in childhood but are harming us now is the way to go ahead.

I'm a firm believer that emotional wellbeing is just as important as breathing. Therapy is essentially a gift, a chance to be heard, understood and supported. People often reach out to therapy when they are in a crisis and because they want something in their life to change. What happens in therapy is undoubtedly important; however the act of reaching out is the biggest act of courage and strength.

Acknowledging that you need help is the first step toward healing and embracing your emotions, is nothing less than an act of bravery. Growing up with the notion that emotions are a weakness and will make you vulnerable to the harsh realities of the world and it's better to live life through a lens of practicality and logic only to realise that being emotionally vulnerable and expressive requires way more strength.

Doctors are often expected to remain composed and professional, even when the emotional impact of a patient's death may be deeply felt. This pressure can cause them to internalize their grief and struggles, as there's often an unspoken expectation that they should not show vulnerability. However, failing to process these emotions can lead to burnout, compassion fatigue, or even depression. This is why talking to someone—whether a colleague, a therapist, or even a family member—can be a vital outlet for doctors to work through their grief and maintain their mental health.

1. Acknowledging Grief: Doctors, like anyone, need space to process their emotions. Losing a patient is not just a clinical event; it's an emotional one. Recognizing that these feelings are normal is crucial.

2. Talking Helps the Process: You feel heard and understood when you eventually confide in a coworker or anybody else with whom you feel at ease. Talking to someone who listens might sometimes be the most therapeutic thing you can do.

3. Self-Care and Support: The example shows the importance of self-care and the need for a support network. Doctors should feel empowered to seek help, whether through therapy or through conversations with trusted colleagues, without fearing judgment.

By encouraging doctors to talk about their emotional struggles, especially after difficult events like patient deaths, healthcare systems can foster healthier, more compassionate work environments and prevent long-term mental health issues that can ultimately affect both doctors and patients.

Breaking the Cycle: A Call to Action

In the end I just want to say that while we may not immediately change the toxic work culture or its demands on our minds and bodies, we can begin fostering change by being kind to ourselves and to those who come after us. Moving forward, let's try to acknowledge our physical, mental and emotional needs and make sure to cater to our inner child before anything else. Life is short, and way too long at the same time, to be spent feeling numb on the inside. Breaking the cycle of poor mental health for doctors is crucial, both for their well-being and the quality of care they provide to patients and there are several strategies that doctors can implement to break this cycle and prioritize their mental health.

1. Recognize the Signs of Burnout Early
2. Build a Support System
3. Engage in Professional Mental Health Support
4. Practice Self-Compassion
5. Set Boundaries
6. Make Time for Physical Health
7. Foster a Culture of Well-being in the Workplace
8. Take Breaks and Use Time Off
9. Focus on the Meaning Behind Your Work
10. Accept That Not Every Outcome Is in Your Control

Final Reflections

To every medical student, doctor, healthcare worker out there, I offer you one of my favourite quotes:- "You carry so much love and kindness in your heart; give some to yourself." Remember to take a step back, breathe and unwind. You're only human. It's a long, long journey, don't forget to enjoy it while chasing your destination. Let's not forget to live our lives and heal ourselves while on this quest to save others.

Because you may be out there trying to save lives, but who is coming to save YOU?

COLORS OF INTERNSHIP

— Dr. Bonny Rishitha Beeda, MBBS,
SVIMS- Sri Padmavathi Medical College for Women, Tirupati, AP, India.

"Take it all one day at a time and enjoy the journey"

— Kristi Bartlett

9

COLORS OF INTERNSHIP

— Dr. Bonny Rishitha Beeda, MBBS,
SVIMS- Sri Padmavathi Medical College for Women, Tirupati, AP, India.

I have always wanted to be a doctor, I didn't have a role model nor did I look up to someone, I just wanted to be a doctor without a reason. I've been a good student throughout med school, and passed out as the best outgoing student of the batch.

Greys anatomy used to be my go to series, I binged on it and bailey and love was my favourite book. I have always wanted to be a surgeon, plastic surgeon or surgical gastroenterologist to be more specific. Then there was my internship which gave me a whole different perspective about life. what changed, did I still want to be a surgeon? Did I become insensitive to mortality?

I started off my internship with internal medicine postings, I was never really fond of medicine. However, something changed in the first 2 months of my internship. I started liking medicine more than I thought I would, I enjoyed the diagnostic workup, I was curious to find the differential diagnosis for the cases. But There were few instances where I questioned the whole work culture in medicine in India. why we had to do night duties and continue doing the morning shift and how doctors never cared about having food on time and end up with gastritis and simply take a pantoprazole like they prescribe to all the patients.

Immediately after medicine I went to my surgery posting,which I thought I would love. As much as I liked suturing, I did not enjoy standing at the OT table and assisting for hours and hours. That's when I started to think that maybe I want medicine more than surgery. I couldn't accept the fact that I was not enjoying surgery cause most of my life I wanted to be a surgeon but on the split side I was rethinking this whole prospect of being a doctor.

This was because I wanted to do many more things in life, I wanted to travel, bake, paint, explore, be adventurous. When I saw my seniors and other doctors I didn't want to be like them, that's not how I would like to see myself in 10 years. So many questions just bombarded me, 5 years of hard work, I didn't have anything against the subject, I loved it, I was always dedicated but it was the work life and medical system was something I was cribbing about.

Internship made me question my whole life, the purpose of it. I was afraid that my 20s would get consumed in medicine, when would I travel? When will I meet more people? When will I live life?

Another burning question for me was if I wanted to continue my studies in India. I have always wanted to study abroad, just for the exposure and cultural exchange. As much as my parents didn't want me to go, I got more stubborn about it. Everything and anything abroad attracted me. I have spent a decent 5 months of my gap year debating if I should go abroad or not. People kept saying that grass is always greener on the other side 2023-24 was the year I introspective, explored and understood myself. I took a gap year after my internship against everyone's advice. I was meant to prepare for my Indian pg entrance exam. However, that one year taught me more than just time management. It taught how to not take life too seriously, how to accept change, how to be spontaneous, how to let go of things, how to look at the bigger picture. Internship is just a teaser to the movie that you'll be seeing in your future, but it sure is fun and is a lifetime experience.

A LIFE OF A DOCTOR: TRIALS, TRIUMPHS, AND THE HUMAN TOUCH

— Dr. Sarakinti Sarika, MBBS,
SVIMS- Sri Padmavathi Medical College for Women, Tirupati, AP, India.

"The awe of discovering the human body. The honor of being trusted to give advice. The gratitude for helping someone through a difficult illness. These things never grow old."

— *Danielle Ofri, MD via The New York Times*

10

A LIFE OF A DOCTOR: TRIALS, TRIUMPHS, AND THE HUMAN TOUCH

— Dr. Sarakinti Sarika, MBBS,
SVIMS- Sri Padmavathi Medical College for Women, Tirupati, AP, India.

Pursuing medicine has been a dream for countless children and students for decades. Of course, I was one of them.

The Journey begins.

It was all good until I achieved a state rank in my 11th and 12th-grade exams. Then the real story began. I couldn't get into my dream undergraduate course—MBBS—and didn't want to waste another year preparing. So, I decided to join BDS (Bachelor of dental surgery) in a government institute.

I wasn't happy. My heart and mind were not at peace. Craving for what I was passionate about. I went through a lot of stress for almost six months. Stress, I mean, an 18-year-old girl about to decide what she's going to do for the rest of her life. It wasn't easy at all. Yet, with a lot of courage, I decided to quit BDS and take a gap year, focusing on the only goal I had at that time.

The Gap Year

It was a year filled with emotions. I didn't know if my decision was right. I wasn't sure if I would crack the national test. I didn't know if the gap year would be worth it, or what I would do if things went wrong. It was stressful. The uncertainty of life hit me hard. The gap year was a period of intense self-reflection. I engaged in activities that helped me understand my strengths, weaknesses, and interests better. This introspection helped me identify areas where I needed to focus my studies and reinforced my commitment to the medical field. Post-exam my score wasn't that good. I landed up with a borderline score and didn't know if I would get into a medical school this time at least. The counselling started. Didn't want to go back to BDS, my family was not financially stable enough to afford a payment category seat, and didn't know if I would get a free seat. Just left things to destiny and awaited the result.

And yes, finally, the dream came true. I got into MBBS—Bachelor of Medicine and Bachelor of Surgery. It all happened in a blink of the eye. I can still feel the joy I shared with my family. My parents were so proud. Until then, life had been all about studies and exams, and I didn't know much about family, friends, the future, or my career.

First steps into the unknown

It was easier when it was just a few books, simple exams, and results. Then came anatomy, physiology, and biochemistry. The words, the sentences, the flowcharts, the cycles, the diagrams, the cadaver, the labs—everything changed all of a sudden. It was all new. Professors started warning us—people's lives are in your hands; keep studying, keep working hard, or else it will be even harder down the road. At that point, it didn't matter much. Medical school is tough. We would only truly understand things once we went through them. That's exactly what happened to me. Attending med school every day of the week except Sundays, from 8 AM to 4 PM. Sacrificing family time, personal time, and social time just to study and do well in med school was far harder than my friends in other fields could understand. At that age, their problems seemed trivial.

Then came our first-year exams—the moment when my friends and I felt like life would end if we didn't pass. So many books. So many volumes. So much to study, so much to remember. I can't even explain how volatile these subjects are. I still remember what I studied in school, but I can't recall what I studied in MBBS. In fact, I can't even recall things I read yesterday. My friends and I were so sure we would fail and have to repeat the year. It was that hard. It pushed us to our limits. But somehow, we all passed.

Stethoscope stories

Then came our clinical postings. The apron and stethoscope on us. It is not as beautiful as it seemed. The anxiety I felt just talking to a patient, touching a patient—I can't describe it in words. With only partial knowledge from our first year, we had to take cases in the hospital. Hospital rounds were tough—not academically, but emotionally and mentally. It's not easy for a young student to witness the pain of patients in a hospital. I used to put myself in their place and carry their pain with me. It was heart-breaking at every step.

Beyond all the medical school challenges, we were also at an age where we had to manage personal relationships, family issues, and our own health. Maybe, it was the start of our adulthood. Extremely difficult phase.

I need to share this part of my story: I once attended a fest with a few friends after a long time. Suddenly, someone pushed me by accident, and my knee twisted. I couldn't stand for two hours. Somehow, with the help of my friends, I managed to get home. The next morning, I woke up with a swollen knee, pain, and an inability to walk. I had to tell my parents I had fallen at the event. My mom took me to the hospital, and after an MRI scan, I was diagnosed with a complete ACL tear, requiring surgery. In an instant, life changed. Of course, anyone with emotions fears surgery and hospital stays. My parents panicked, and I broke down in tears. I couldn't imagine myself unable to walk and do my best. I wasn't in a position to explain to them or give them any hope that everything would be okay. After a week, we decided to go ahead with the surgery, and it took me nearly three months to recover to normal life. Those three months were the hardest and taught me so many things: the value of my body, my health, and the support of my family. I strongly believe that any doctor who has already been a patient and gone through the pain in a hospital knows what his/her patient is going through. I cried aloud when they gave me spinal anaesthesia. The pain was unbearable. Using a walker to go out or just to get down from bed was very depressing. I completely recovered and strengthened my knee after a lot of challenges.

COVID19—another life-changing period. People around started panicking. Everybody behaved like strangers because of the fear of COVID transmission even if they talk to somebody for a second. Few of them started blaming doctors for not being there with the patients 24/7. There was this scarcity of hospital beds all over the world. Barren lands turned into graveyards. To have loved ones who take good care of you at the hardest point is a bliss. A friend of mine lost her dad to COVID who was the only earner in the family and she was 19 then. Our village lost its soul residents. It was all scary. I didn't personally experience much loss, but the stories I heard from friends and family were terrifying. Eventually, it all ended somehow.

The final curtain

The most engaging, yet challenging. ENT, Ophthalmology, public health sciences, general medicine. General surgery, obstetrics and gynaecology, paediatrics. Time to learn the actual things to practice.

Another story of mine is here.

With all the stress, I started binge eating more often. Health didn't matter much at that age compared to my medical school and personal responsibilities. I was just like any other student. Then, I gave a blood sample for a senior's research, and the results showed that my random blood sugars were 220 mg/dl, and fasting sugars were 140 mg/dl. I was 20 years old. I didn't know what to do. I just stopped junk for a while. I didn't consult a doctor. I was obese and feared being scolded for not checking on my health as a medico. I couldn't tell my parents either. Eventually, I decided to get a HbA1c test, and the result was 10%, which is clearly very abnormal for a 20-year-old. I finally told one of my uncles, who was a doctor, and he started me on medication and advised me to engage in physical activity. We didn't have much time for ourselves, but eventually, things got better. I was on medication and didn't check my sugar levels often. I just hoped it would all turn normal one day. I continued with my pre-final and final years and managed to pass all my exams. That was one of the happiest moments for all of us.

On the front lines

Being a student under the guidance of professors is very different from being a doctor and treating patients. It's a new phase of life. A profession—great and noble—but also mentally and physically challenging. As a student, we had the opportunity to take leaves when we weren't okay. But as an intern, that was no longer the case. We had to work, no matter our personal situation. We had to save lives and give people hope.

It's not easy to smile and give hope to patients when personal problems are running through your head. It's not easy to not relate our own struggles to the patients' experiences. It's not easy to put ourselves at risk of communicable diseases. It's not easy to work endless hours. It's not easy to sacrifice family, sleep, health, food, and social time to save others. It's not easy to stay calm amidst chaos. It's not easy to watch someone die in your hands. It's not easy to watch someone cry over their loved ones. And it's certainly not easy to go home and pretend everything is fine after all of this. I couldn't accept the fact that this would be my life forever. Slowly, everything changed. I started accepting that it's okay to push myself hard if it means someone else gets the chance to live. It was a hard realization, but it took time. The internship, though challenging, was one of the most beautiful phases of my life. I learned so much, and by the time I grew to love the work, it was already over.

Charting the course

I don't know. The mental turmoil I went through in deciding what to do next is hard to explain. After a lot of suggestions and help from my family, I decided to prepare for the USMLE, weighing the pros and cons. But then, financial troubles at home hit. My father is over 60, and I couldn't ask him to work and support the family. It was my turn to take over. I found a job to help cover the family's expenses, but I couldn't find the time to study for my exams. Balancing work, studies, and family was incredibly difficult.

On a positive note, I began focusing on my health. I started working on my diabetes, exercising regularly, and eating clean. It's been eight months now, and my HbA1c has come down to 5.6%.

Currently, I'm navigating this phase of life, and I'm happy to have grown to a point where I can manage everything.

This is just my story, and there are countless other doctors with equally difficult stories. We go through a lot, both professionally and personally. The very difficult part of being a doctor is managing mental health. Acknowledge your struggles, seek support, and make time for self-care. Balance your professional responsibilities with personal well-being. Remember, a healthy mind enables you to provide the best care to others.

HOW MUCH FREEDOM IS TOO MUCH FREEDOM?

— *Dr. Venkata Sai Deepthi Rayadurgam, MBBS,*
SVIMS- Sri Padmavathi Medical College for Women, Tirupati, AP, India.

"The best way to predict the future is to CREATE it."

— Peter Drucker

11

HOW MUCH FREEDOM IS TOO MUCH FREEDOM?

— Dr. Venkata Sai Deepthi Rayadurgam, MBBS,
SVIMS- Sri Padmavathi Medical College for Women, Tirupati, AP, India.

What If I Had Never Stepped Out of My Comfort Zone?

Sitting on my terrace with a hot cup of coffee, watching the sun dip below the horizon, I can't help but think about my MBBS days. Five and a half years of pure chaos—excitement, rebellion, laughter, and life lessons. How on earth did I survive those years? If I could go back and give my younger self one piece of advice, it would be this: cherish the freedom college brings because it shapes you in ways nothing else can.I was 17 when I stepped into medical college—a shy girl from an orthodox family, suddenly surrounded by strangers. My first challenge? Make friends. But how? Should I introduce myself? What if I said something weird? Finally,during our lab session, I awkwardly said hello —and that hello turned into friendships that I am grateful for even today.

Did We Push the Limits Too Far? Or Was It the Only Way to Learn?

As time passed, I found my voice, made decisions, and embraced independence. Slowly, I drifted from my parents—not intentionally, but because I was discovering myself. My friends and I shared an adventurous spirit, and life became thrilling. Doesn't that sound like the beginning of something unforgettable?

Take one Saturday, for example. After our first lecture, my friends and I impulsively decided to bunk the rest of the day and visit a lake far from college. The sun was shining, the breeze was perfect, and the thrill of skipping class made it all the more exciting. Did we tell our parents? Of course not! That would ruin the fun. Standing by the calm, sparkling lake, rebellion and euphoria coursed through our veins. At that moment, we felt unbeatable. Until, of course, we got home and faced our moms wraths. But secretly? We were proud. we had taken a risk and pulled it off. Did we really make it worth it? Say a memory that would stay with us forever? Yes. Absolutely. It was worth it.These moments remind me to ask you: When was the last time you chose adventure over routine? Would you have a story to tell if you didn't?

What Do You Do When Everything Goes Wrong?

Then came the ultimate adventure—and a terrifying one. We had planned to attend a prestigious conference at JIPMER, Pondicherry. The plan was perfect: three days of conference, followed by beaches, cafes, and sightseeing. What could go wrong? Apparently, everything. On the day of our return, disaster struck. We realized we had lost the address of the bike rental shop, where our licenses and IDs were still held. Three hours left before our bus, dead phones, no map, and panic set in. What do you do when you're stuck in a strange city with no idea where to go?Oh, and to make things worse, two strangers started following us. Were they thieves? Were we imagining it? Was this a crime thriller we hadn't signed up for?Helpless we were. My mind raced— why didn't we save the address? Why didn't we double-check our plans? But panicking wasn't helping. So, what now? Should I cry? Should I run? Should I pretend this isn't happening?Finally, a kind family came to our rescue, patiently drawing a route map on paper (old-school, right?). Luckily, we found the shop just in time and made it to our bus, sweaty, exhausted, and relieved. That small act of kindness gave us hope, and within minutes, we were on the right track. Through all this chaos, the best part was my friends. We were a balanced team:

- One was the daring risk-taker.
- Another was calm and composed.
- One was the planner who prepared us for consequences.
- And one brought humor to every situation. Together, we pushed each other out of our comfort zones while always having each other's backs.

And here's the funny part: we now laugh about that day, calling it our "Pondy Survival Episode." That's the thing about life—it's messy, unpredictable, and sometimes scary. When you think of those memories in the long run, they become the best stories and the biggest lessons.So next time you're stuck in chaos, remember: Stay calm, stay curious, and stay hopeful. After all, what's an adventure without a little drama?

Is Freedom More About Connection Than Rebellion?

Not all our escapades were chaotic, though. One of my favorite memories was a spontaneous sleepover at a friend's house. We cooked dinner following a YouTube tutorial, laughing at our disastrous attempts. We danced, watched our favorite series, and talked for hours about everything and nothing. That night, I realized freedom isn't just about rebellion—it's also about finding joy in small, simple moments with the people who matter.

Is Freedom Still the Same When Responsibility Kicks In?

Life took a serious turn during my internship. The freedom I once took for granted came with immense responsibility. Night duties as a "doctor" felt surreal. Walking the hospital's dark corridors, my white coat trailing behind, I tried to look confident—even when I wasn't. Exhaustion became normal, and my mind became a storage house for drug names and patient histories. But in between those sleepless nights, there were victories—tiny but fulfilling. Inserting my first cannula, handling my first case, calming a restless patient. Still, we found ways to make it fun. Tea breaks in the canteen became sacred rituals, where we laughed at how pharmacology used to scare us or shared our horror stories from duty. Midnight drives and eating dosa at 3 AM reminded us of what freedom felt like—even if it lasted for a short period of time.But were we misusing that freedom? Skipping lectures, sneaking past hostel security, bending rules—were these just reckless acts, or were they the very lessons that taught us about limits?Internship taught me the true meaning of responsible freedom. It's thrilling to break free, but freedom without responsibility can be chaos. It's about finding balance—enjoying life while staying true to your duties.

The Final Takeaway: "No Regrets, Just Lessons—The Real Price of Freedom"

Being a huge fan of the sitcom How I Met Your Mother, I would like to quote few of my favorite lines by Ted Mosby(the lead character):

"You can't just skip ahead to where you think your life should be. The journey is the best part."

A reminder that life isn't about rushing to the destination; it's about embracing every step along the way.

"Funny how sometimes you just find things."

This reflects how life often leads us to exactly what we need, even when we're not looking for it.

"Sometimes things need to fall apart to make way for better things."

A powerful reminder that life often works through setbacks and failures to lead us to where we're meant to be.

Remember, we often stress about planning every step, mapping out the perfect path, and controlling every outcome. But in reality, some of the best things in life happen by accident—the friendships that form unexpectedly, the lessons we never saw coming, the risks we never planned to take but somehow ended up shaping us.Destiny has a strange way of guiding us, even when we feel lost.

As I sip my coffee now, watching the sky turn orange, I feel nothing but gratitude—for the mistakes, the risks, the adventures, and the friendships.If I could go back, would I change anything? Not a chance. I'd probably do it all over again.And to you, dear younger me, my junior —what will freedom mean to you? Will you take risks, learn, and grow, or let it slip by unnoticed?

The choice is yours.

FROM MY INTERNSHIP JOURNAL!

— *Dr. Yuvakeerthana Ramachandra, MBBS,*
SVIMS- Sri Padmavathi Medical College for Women, Tirupati, AP, India.

"The mind is everything. What you think, you become".

— *Gautam Buddha*

12

FROM MY INTERNSHIP JOURNAL!

— Dr. Yuvakeerthana Ramachandra, MBBS,
SVIMS- Sri Padmavathi Medical College for Women, Tirupati, AP, India.

Embarking on an internship in the medical field is an experience filled with challenges, growth, and invaluable lessons. Over the course of my time as an intern, I encountered a myriad of situations that tested my skills, resilience, and emotional fortitude. Each department brought its own unique experiences, shaping me not only as a medical professional but also as an individual. Here, I share some of the most memorable and impactful moments from my internship, illustrating the highs and lows that have left an indelible mark on my journey.

An Episode from Emergency Department

It was 8am in the morning and I was waiting for my reliever to come so that I could finally get some rest. I had just finished my night duty at the Emergency Department. As my reliever arrived I went back to the hostel to get some sleep. Unlike before,this time my sleep had a background music score banging in my head, just like the BGM in the movies.I just could not unhear those noises-the rhythmic hospital sounds of a heart monitor, ICU mechanical ventilator, IV pumps, sisters yelling at the staff, asking to put some cannulas, Ryles tubes, injections for patients, and so on.

After my fortnight Radiology posting, this was my first clinical department in my internship.I was so elated that I kept doing all the work that came my way, just like any other intern excited for their clinical postings. I used to jot down all the do's, don'ts and medications that residents would tell me. The initial adrenaline rush pushed me to do so.

Everything was going well until the time I was supposed to communicate with people. It was tough to talk to patient attenders, especially in EMD. Tackling the attenders of brought dead patients was a challenge; dealing with their behaviour was yet another tedious task.People would dump all their ill will, yell, and whatnot! But at the end of the day, that's how human emotions are…..can't blame anyone.

The Hard Realities

It was hard for me to spill the facts and yet be sensible,and the hardest was aligning with things that were blatantly wrong. Learning things at the verge of someone else's life felt so compassionless and that disturbed me, but that's how things work sometimes. I went into a negativity spiral for a period. Amidst all the chaos, watching sick patients feel relieved gave me a break from all that mental fuzziness.

Emergency medicine posting in a nutshell, was no less than a horror film for me. I was longing to leave this department at the earliest possible. But after a "vent session" with my friend, I realised the brighter side of it & the sense of satisfaction I gained from being there.

Moments of Gratitude

I truly enjoyed the experience and learnt a lot from it as well. The wholesome moments when people thanked us with gratitude while we untangle the knot of pain are what we cherish. Doing repeated CPR cycles in the hope of reviving a patient has driven me to become an optimistic person. Handling cases nonchalantly was a challenge, and I am still in the process of learning to be calmer in such challenging situations, which is tough though!

A Changed Perspective

EMD has definitely changed my perspective on life.It taught me to look at situations in a lighter, more logical, and cooler way rather than being tense.I tried leading my life in a solution based manner without getting stuck there. I also started finding some entertainment in anything and everything during heavy times, and that's when things didn't seem to burden me.

A Glimpse from Ortho

Orthopaedics posting was a theatre of depression for me where I had to grab all the tickets in there. In Fact the only part that kept me sane was the OT complex. The best part was having my name on the list of surgeons performing operations on the OT writing board, even though I was just an intern assisting the surgery. I could find some calmness there. All the lavish OTs had my heart; I enjoyed and loved being there. Two weeks into the postings, I was left with a day where I literally prayed for some miracle to happen before I left the department because I was all upset and had no sense of satisfaction in all those days.Luckily, I was grateful enough to assist a visiting surgeon for three back-to-back surgeries.That's when I finally felt the purpose of being there. The surgeon was so chivalrous and mindful of what he was doing.

All the surgeries went smoothly, and I was blessed to hear all the insights from him. He saintly said a few words that actually influenced me. From my very tender age I was a devotee of LORD RAMA! I always considered "The Ramayana" as our history rather than a mere mythological tale. I was overwhelmed when he shared exactly the same with me. I was kind of impressed and could relate to many other points as well. I was also happy and thankful when he appreciated my work. It will forever remain a delightful memory for my life.

The Paediatric Moments: Unexpected Joys

Well, the only posting I was reluctant to go was paeds because, I am not a great fan of kids, especially toddlers. I find them so annoying. To my surprise, I found some cute & fond memories there. The kids waving their hands while they got discharged, infants grabbing our fingers, all these moments were so precious. Here I tell the story of a father waiting outside the ICU to grab his baby girl in his arms on the day of her discharge from the hospital. The baby girl was 5 days old and sick. Her father used to visit her every now and then but hesitated to touch or carry her. Her mother was also so weak that she was admitted to the obstetrics and gynaecology ward. I also noticed that he wore the same clothes every day. He used to be always at the door, would come in to watch his kid and leave. I once asked him to freshen up and change clothes, assuring him that we would look after his kid well. With all humbleness on his face,he refused to do so because he had no money to spare for new clothes. All he had with him was another pair of clothes that he kept it to wear on the day of his child's discharge. He told me that since his wife was weak, he was supposed to carry his daughter on the day of discharge, so he saved the clothes to wear on that day so that his daughter would not get infected. And the moment he gently took his daughter into his arms, the smile on his face made my day. All I could do was just admire them and cherish that moment. This is one of the fondest memories I have.

The Surgery times: From Scalpel to Sutures

Scrubs, Scalpel & Surgeon.... I would go crazy for these words. I was always fascinated to be called a surgeon and was on cloud nine when residents addressed me in that way! (In reality they just chose the nicer way to get the work done). As an enthusiastic intern, I was manifesting to have a scalpel in hand,make my first incision, and put in sutures. I was so very happy when I got those chances. The day I made my first incision will always remain as a special moment. As the OT complex had always been my favourite place, the majority of my memories were also from there. It feels exhilarating when you scrub in and enter an operation theatre! Of course most of the time as an intern, you just hold retractors and stand with no idea what you're contributing at, but I used to wait for that rare moment when surgeon would give us sutures to close, while anaesthetist insists 'not to', and it hits differently, by the way.

I once encountered something engaging: most of the surgeons are sarcastic. I truly do not know whether people who are actually witty get into this department or choose to be so after getting into residency.However I used to thoroughly vibe around them. The surgical experiences they shared were so satisfying to hear. Nevertheless hard times are inevitable in any posting, but it did not seem that way this time. Probably, pleasure in work at your favourite place doesn't burden you. Learning different suturing techniques and knotting methods from residents was my favourite part. There was this one time during this posting, where I learned something valuable apart from the subject and the work from one of the residents: the so-called "Willpower".

An elderly man was battling for his survival at the intensive care unit. Everyone was already sure that he would collapse in an hour or so despite all the best efforts. But to our surprise, he held his breath until the next day. Be it a second, an hour, or a day, he didn't give up. This experience taught me to have a stubborn heart and unwavering determination to keep going until the end. I never imagined the final year of my medical school would be this memorable and transformative. By consistently believing in myself and focusing on tasks, even those I initially doubted I could do, I witnessed remarkable improvement. This journey has significantly evolved my mindset. Our mind holds immense power in shaping our reality, and with persistent effort and the right mindset, we can achieve great things.

REDEFINING DREAMS: A STORY OF COURAGE AND RESILIENCE

— Dr. A R Chaitanya, MBBS, MD,

MD Pulmonary Medicine; fellowship - Diploma in Asthma and Allergy (CMC VELLORE), Ex-assistant professor (SVIMS), India.

"Life is like topography, Hobbes. There are summits of happiness and success, flat stretches of boring routine and valleys of frustration and failure."

— *Bill waterson*

13

REDEFINING DREAMS: A STORY OF COURAGE AND RESILIENCE

— Dr. A R Chaitanya, MBBS, MD,
MD Pulmonary Medicine; fellowship - Diploma in Asthma and Allergy
(CMC VELLORE), Ex-assistant professor (SVIMS), India.

It was another routine day in the outpatient clinic. As a pulmonologist, I expected the usual cases—asthma, COPD, tuberculosis. Nothing out of the ordinary.

The knock on my door broke the monotony. A woman entered, accompanied by a man and a boy in a wheelchair. The boy was thin yet well-built, his face was a mix of enthusiasm and anxiety. A tracheostomy tube protruded from his neck.

For a fleeting moment, my mind raced through possible diagnoses—Guillain-Barré syndrome? Multidrug-resistant pneumonia? Prolonged ventilation? Before I could settle on a theory, the mother spoke.

"Hello, doctor," she greeted me. "We've been referred by the ENT specialist for his tracheostomy removal."

I nodded, suppressing my immediate flood of questions. Instead, I started with my usual small talk.

"Where are you from?"

She answered.

"How many children do you have?"

"Two sons. He's my elder one."

I was still piecing things together. "And what do you do for a living?"

"I'm a daily laborer," she replied.

Finally, I asked the real question. "What happened?"

She smiled—an unexpected expression for such a situation. "He fell from an under-construction two-story building without railings." The fall has resulted in the spinal injury leading to paralysis of both lower limbs.

I glanced at the boy, then back at her. "When?"

"A month ago."

Turning to the boy, I asked, "Which grade were you in?"

Before he could respond, his mother stepped in, but he gestured with his fingers—five plus four. Ninth grade.

"What were you doing up there?"

The boy raised his hand slightly and whispered through the tracheostomy tube, "Playing kabaddi with friends."

I looked at his mother. "You didn't see him go up?"

She shook her head. "I usually keep an eye on him, but it was early morning. I asked him to study while I was cooking for his school lunch. He sneaked out in between."

I continued taking his history, reviewing his chest X-ray in the lobby. As I stood to examine him, I asked, "What do you want to be when you grow up?"

For the first time in our conversation, silence filled the room. The mother's ever-present smile faltered, if only for a second.

"He always wanted to be an army officer," she finally said, her voice softer now. "But now… he can't."

The boy, undeterred, made a typing motion with his fingers. I frowned, confused. His mother translated, "Now he wants to become a software engineer."

I turned back to him. "How good are you in school?"

He held up a hand—first and second. Always at the top of his class.

I smiled, pulling open my drawer and handing him a pen. "Then keep studying. You'll do great."

He gave me a thumbs-up.

Two things from that day remained etched in my memory—the unwavering smile of his mother, except for that single fleeting moment of sadness, and the boy's resilience, his quiet determination in the face of life's unexpected turns.

And here I was, worrying about my next publication, job uncertainties, and my meager salary.

Life has a way of teaching us what truly matters. Get up. Dust yourself off. Face the next challenge with a smile and a thumbs-up.

A Doctor's First Night – The Pride Shattered

After the announcement of the final MBBS Part 2 results, it was a moment of triumph, victory, and pride—for both me and my parents. Yet again, I had secured a medal in Obstetrics and Gynaecology. Winning a medal had become a ritual every year of MBBS, and the final year was no exception. Finally, I was a doctor—though I had yet to receive my registration or license to practice. The excitement of being addressed as "doctor" by nurses and patients, walking through the wards with a newfound sense of responsibility, was overwhelming.

Adding to the significance of the day, it was my birthday and also my first day as an intern—the beginning of my journey as a doctor. Everything was new—the patients, the responsibility of monitoring vitals, and the long hours. In Indian government medical colleges, where the workload is high and the number of doctors is low, interns are often entrusted with critical tasks early on. That night, I was assigned to monitor a patient with acute pancreatitis in the emergency department. I knew from theory that hypotension is a common complication and that when the radial pulse is feeble, the carotid pulse is a better indicator of blood volume. While recording the patient's blood pressure every two hours, I noticed that I couldn't feel his radial pulse. Hesitant and unsure, I attempted to palpate his carotid pulse.

A surgery resident, who had been observing me before heading for dinner at 11 PM, paused and asked why I was checking the carotid pulse. Nervously, I explained that the radial pulse was weak. Without hesitation, she rushed in, secured a large-bore IV cannula, and started fluids to improve the patient's blood pressure. Within half an hour, she left for dinner, leaving me and another resident in charge of the entire casualty department.

Shortly after, a call came from the ward: a terminally ill patient on palliative care was deteriorating. Since my senior resident was needed in casualty, I was sent to assess the patient. The surgery resident had already explained that nothing much could be done—just the "masterly inactivity" we were taught. I walked through the dark hospital corridors to reach the ward. By the time I arrived, the patient had suffered a cardiac arrest, and a code blue had been activated. CPR was already in progress.

At that moment, all the Basic Life Support (BLS) and Advanced Cardiac Life Support (ACLS) theories flashed through my mind. The nurse's voice jolted me from my thoughts, and I quickly grabbed gloves to assist with CPR. After multiple cycles, the inevitable task fell upon me—I had to declare the patient dead. The ECG was flat, heart sounds had ceased, there was no chest rise, no air entry into the lungs, and the pupils were dilated and unresponsive. The nurse encouraged me to formally announce the death. Apprehensive and anxious, I hesitated, but with their support, I managed to complete the task. Writing the death summary, however, was an entirely different challenge—far removed from the textbook formats. Overwhelmed, I handed the responsibility to my senior resident.

Just as I thought the night's ordeal was over, another call came—from the surgery ward. A nurse reported that a patient had climbed the compound wall and was wandering around, disturbing others. Exhausted and sleep-deprived after working since 8 AM, I struggled to think clearly. Upon reaching the ward, I found a man admitted for a foot ulcer, now confused and rambling about "ketchup being poured" over his wound, which was just betadine staining. He was also trembling. When I called my senior, he asked if the patient was an alcoholic. On inquiry, I confirmed that the man was a chronic drinker who had been deprived of alcohol since admission. The diagnosis was clear—alcohol withdrawal. Treatment was initiated accordingly.

At 2 AM, drained and sleepless, I walked back with a heavy heart and 10 more hours of duty left. My sense of triumph had faded, replaced by exhaustion and introspection.

That night, I realized the vast difference between theory and practice, between textbook cases and real human beings. I learned that every patient, even with the same disease, presents uniquely. Most of all, I understood that declaring a death is not just a protocol—it is an art, and one of the most difficult lessons a doctor must learn. The pride of my medals seemed insignificant now. If anything, I had grasped one harsh truth—true excellence requires relentless hard work, and I still had a long way to go.

YOUR JOURNEY WITH MEDICINE

— Dr. Shriramya. M, MBBS, MD,
MBBS (JIPMER), MD Medicine (SVIMS), Fellowship in Diabetology, India.

"Follow the Master

Face the Devil

Fight to the end

Finish the Game"

— Bhagawan Sri Sathya Sai Baba

14

YOUR JOURNEY WITH MEDICINE

— Dr. Shriramya. M, MBBS, MD,
MBBS (JIPMER), MD Medicine (SVIMS), Fellowship in Diabetology, India.

An intricate art
That makes you stand apart
A science quite old
That can't be bought or sold
To see with the hand
To try and understand
To hear with the mind
The clockwork behind
To follow the dogma
Solve many an enigma
To study the illness, its course
And try and treat the source
All your youth you will train
For the skills you must gain
You will study hard and deep
To get a prefix to keep
Your transformation is a treasure
That only you can measure
People close and far
Will see you as their star
Some times are testing
When you work without resting
But those who come your way

Live to see another day
Experience will show
How to apply what you know
There is a lot you know to do
But must know when not to
We see case after case
Keep running our own race
But when we slow down our pace
We see the fear, the face
Your word makes them calm
Your voice, a soothing balm
For both the strong and the weak
It is love that they seek
You prescribe the cure
But with your touch, you ensure
For what is swallowed is the pill
But what heals is the will

– Dr. Shriramya.M

MED SCHOOL: A DESTINATION OF LIFE LESSONS (BEYOND THE CLASSROOM)

— Dr. Sree Sritha, Nellore, MBBS,
SVIMS- Sri Padmavathi Medical College for Women, Tirupati, AP, India.

*"Always walk through life as if you have something new to learn,
and you will."*

– Vernon Howard

15

MED SCHOOL: A DESTINATION OF LIFE LESSONS (BEYOND THE CLASSROOM)

— Dr. Sree Sritha, Nellore, MBBS,
SVIMS- Sri Padmavathi Medical College for Women, Tirupati, AP, India.

Hello there! After reading the title, you might be wondering how medschool could be teaching life lessons in addition to lessons about life within our bodies. But trust me, it does. And they happen not just in the classroom, but beyond it too. I'm going to take you guys with me into my med school days where I learned lessons that helped me grow as a person and made me the compassionate and principled doctor that I am today.

We Listen and We Don't Judge

Med School is a place where we are taught not just 'how to treat patients' but also 'how to look at them' During my 2nd year of MBBS, in my clinical posting of General Medicine, Dr. Bhargav, who was an associate professor back then, taught us values that I will treasure throughout my life. Sir's words - "I was in the OP yesterday, and I came across a patient who was an alcoholic. I inquired what his profession was. He said he was a drain cleaner. That explained his habit of consuming alcohol. Just imagine yourselves walking next to an open drain. You would feel disgusted by the smell, cover your nose and mouth or just walk away from it. Now, imagine this man's situation, where it is his everyday job to go deep into the drainage canals and clean them despite the horrible smell and the possible risk of infection. He does this not just because it's his job to do so, but to make it safer and cleaner for all of us. This explains why he was consuming alcohol at work.

He was using the numbing effect of alcohol to overcome the difficulties and disgust in his job. What you need to understand here is - I could have just judged the patient, labeled him as alcoholic in my mind, and could have given treatment in a biased frame of mind. But judging him is not my job, treating him is. This is what you all need to remember - 'YOU ARE NOT HERE TO JUDGE THE PATIENT. YOU ARE HERE TO TREAT HIM'. Because you don't know what he is going through." These words struck me like lightning. That day I decided - This is how I'm going to 'look at' and treat my patients.

Later on, I realised that this notion of NON JUDGEMENTAL-MINDSET could be applied to life in general. We need not judge anybody at all. We just need to fulfil our role in our relationships and interactions. If we are in the role of lending money to someone, we just need to do so. If our near and dear are in need of emotional support, we just need to extend warmth and support. We do not have to judge them for anything - not their helplessness, not their behaviour, not their life choices. Because we don't know what they are going through and what their life story is all about.

Down the line, I came across a patient who was diagnosed with syphilis, a sexually transmitted disease. I started thinking in terms of the stage of syphilis the patient was in and the treatment that could cure the condition. Not even once had a judgmental thought crossed my mind. This is when I realised that the lesson I had learned was showing an impact on me. I was elated by this transformation in my thinking. I thanked Dr. Bhargav in my heart for making me a better person and a better doctor. I will always be grateful for this change that sir brought in me. Now, I keep sharing this advice to all people near and dear to me and I ask them to implement it in their lives. I am asking you, dear reader, to do the same thing. I guarantee you that you will experience a lot of joy and peace in your life.

As Dedicated As a Doctor

I was in my internship when this incident happened. I was doing a night shift in the ICU. The doctor in charge was Dr. Vijay, a 3rd year General Medicine resident and I was the intern on duty. Before going for his dinner break, he called out to me and said, "Sritha, I'll be gone for an hour. Please do not hesitate to call me regarding any patient - be it a minor issue or an emergency. Because, to me, my patient's well being is the most important thing. Everything else- my food, my break are secondary to my patient's well being. No patient should go sick under my watch. Understood?"

This was a moment of inspiration to me. This is when I realised how dedicated doctors are towards their patients, and how dedicated they should be, because it is human lives that they are dealing with. I again saw an analogy to life. If every person is dedicated and devoted to what they do and what they need to do, the world would be a better place for all of us. If you are dedicated as a doctor, no patient will go ill; if you are dedicated as an engineer, there will be sturdy buildings for generations to come. This applies to relationships too. If you are dedicated as a parent, you will be able to shape young minds into responsible individuals. If you are dedicated as a friend, you will never let your friends step into dangerous paths.

As I started applying this into my life, I started experiencing immense satisfaction in my work as well as in my personal life. When I was working as an intern in the General Medicine ward, I used to work beyond my shift to make sure that I completed the notes, sent samples to the lab, finished transfusions and all the paperwork that was assigned to me. This actually gave me a great amount of happiness and satisfaction at work. Even in my personal life, I try to go the extra mile by dedicating my time, energy, resources and whatever possible, to just see a smile on the face of my parents and friends. And trust me, you have no idea how much it means to me to just see them smile. And the effort I put in for it just vanishes away. So this is what Vijay sir and I would say - "BE AS DEDICATED AS A DOCTOR IN ALL WALKS OF LIFE."

Friends - The Unsung Teachers

FRIENDS - the souls that make us feel alive and young, the hearts that make us feel loved and special, the shoulders that wipe our tears and extend warmth, the hands that hold us tight and never let us feel alone, the feet that walk with us in all walks of life, the ears that hear us out with no judgement, the lockers where our secrets are kept safe, and the people who stick with us through thick and thin.

However, this is not the end of a friend's role in our lives. They play a major role in shaping us into the people we are. They are the actual UNSUNG TEACHERS in our life. We usually do not acknowledge their role as teachers, because most of the classes happen unintentionally. They don't teach us, we learn from them, and we learn by transmission. This transmission occurs as we laugh together, eat together, sleep together, and literally live together for a grand five and a half years.

In my Med School, I was blessed to have a wonderful group of people whom I could call FRIENDS. We were a gang of six and we called ourselves the "BEEHIVE". I also had a friend outside this gang. All of them were amazing individuals. As much as we loved and cared for each other, we also gave each other space. We were vigilant of each other's misguided choices, while making sure that we did not puppet each other's lives. This is when I started understanding the concept of HEALTHY BOUNDARIES. And again, I started realising that this could be applied to everybody and in all parts of life. Communicating your boundaries and understanding the other person's boundaries is key to a healthy relationship, be it personal or at work. There would be no place for suffocation and exhaustion, there would only be space, time and joy where one can focus on their own personal growth and also help the other person grow. This happened in our story too. We could focus on ourselves and also lend a hand to others.

Now I would like to throw some limelight on my lovely UNSUNG TEACHERS, who made my life better and became the friends that turned into family:

We had an embodiment of Love in our gang, Pooja. She taught us that while being true to our loved ones is important, it is equally important to be true to ourselves. And that, while it is essential to spend time and take care of your loved ones, it is necessary to give ourselves the time, space and love that we deserve. She handles situations like nobody else. She is a strong support system for our gang. She is our go-to person for anything and everything. She is a person that we can count on at any point in life. This is all because she makes us feel that way. And this is something we love in her and learn from her.

Then there was our quirky couch potato, Farheen. We used to admire how strong she was emotionally (we rarely ever saw her feeling sad or tears rolling down her eyes). I really loved her self-sufficient mindset(she hardly ever asked people for help; she used to manage most of her matters alone). We were always amused by her ability to be emotionally detached while still loving and being loved.

Pooja and Farheen were my roommates throughout med school, and I was lucky to have them in my life. They were my support system. They taught me a lot - doing chores, handling people, saying 'no' and many more life skills that I will cherish throughout my existence. They helped me survive and thrive in hostel life, which I was experiencing for the first time. I will always be grateful to them.

We also had a crazy but caring, hasty but smart and lazy but close to the heart, lass in the gang. She is Vaishnavi, the girl with an amazing perspective. In her view, a fight or an argument between two people is just a heated conversation when they have opposing perspectives towards a certain aspect of life. It is not something that pushes people apart, but instead pulls them together because it gives a better understanding of each other's perspectives(once they discuss it after the heat of the argument comes down). She has also been my roommate for two years. We share a similar kind of thinking called OVERTHINKING. So it was easier for us to resonate, relate, communicate, bind and empathize. It was also easier to share our insights and advice on different aspects of life. We share a really close bond between us.

We had a gorgeous diva in the gang, named Hasya. She was beautiful inside and out. She taught us how to love people and cherish friendships while still giving ourselves adequate priority. We also learned from her how to be independent. She threw light on various opportunities and extra-academic activities that we were totally unaware of. She is a person we look up to. She is still our consultant when it comes to matters like beauty, travel, technology, emotional stability and relationship advice(includes all kinds of relationships, not just the one you are thinking of).

We also had an affectionate and compassionate buddy, Aruna. From her, we learned that we have to stand for our families when they are in need of us, no matter what our situation or emotional status is. Because family is more important than anything else in the world. We saw her doing this at a young age. We have also seen her taking up family responsibilities at a young age. We always respect her for this.

Another one of us is a bubbly and sweet pal, Sreeja. She was my partner in the lab, postings as well as duties. She is proof that sharing does not deprive you; instead, it endows you with joy and even expands what we have, especially when it comes to aspects like knowledge and information. She also taught me that a disturbance between two people is just a knot in the thread, not a break in it. I will always admire her for this lesson.

My friends have a huge impact on me. They guided me in the past, they continue to shape me now, and I am pretty sure that they will stand by me to give advice in the future. I will always be thankful to them for influencing me in the way they did.

These are some of the life lessons I learned from my professors, seniors and my buddies during my precious time in med school. I am forever indebted to them for making me the person I am today. Lastly, my advice to medical students is - Keep your eyes and mind open, you may get life lessons from anywhere in med school, both in and out of the classroom. HAPPY LEARNING!!

SCARS, SCRUBS AND SURVIVAL

— Dr. S. Sreeja, MBBS,
SVIMS- Sri Padmavathi Medical College for Women, Tirupati, AP, India.

"The greatest battles are fought within the silent chambers of one's own soul"

— David O. Mckay

16

SCARS, SCRUBS AND SURVIVAL

— Dr. S. Sreeja, MBBS,
SVIMS- Sri Padmavathi Medical College for Women, Tirupati, AP, India.

Dear reader,

If you think this is just another typical "I wanna be a doctor and save lives" story, Think again. This isn't about a genius prodigy who always knew she was destined for medicine. This is about a girl full of curiosity and ambitions, yet packed with flaws,fears and self doubt. A girl who survived her toughest mental challenges…Well, there's a silver lining…that girl had some amazing moments of joy, laughter and friendships too.

So where do I start?

I was a kid who was extremely curious about everything and loved studying and learning new things. Everything was a challenge and a game to win. I tried to win every game, I mean every exam, every weekend test I wrote. Well, I mostly won, and when I failed, those failures hit me hard, knocking the air out of my lungs. However, I harbor no regrets as I loved every minute of it.

The day I got into med school, my family celebrated. And me? I felt nothing, no overwhelming joy, no tears of happiness. I don't know why but I just packed my bags, and was ready for a new city. Excited? Very much. Little did I know that city was about to change me in ways I never saw coming.

Enter the dragon. First day of Med School, in the Anatomy Dissection Hall, was my first time seeing a dead body. My heart raced a little, but my curiosity always won over my fear, so without hesitation, I uncovered the cadaver and saw it. A pale lifeless form lay before me. It felt slightly creepy, but it was fine. I sat on a stool and checked out all the new faces. That's when the professor asked, "Who wants to volunteer?" Most of the girls raised their hands,but I didn't. How could I? I didn't even know the rules of the game I was playing. But as I sat there watching all the enthusiasm around me, I realized, all the girls surrounding me were highly capable and studious and it would be difficult to win this game and I thought to myself," I have to be ready!" But life wasn't what i expected.

Anatomy of a broken spirit

I had some friends once. I liked them. I really did. But there were differences between us. We fought, I made a few mistakes, and they did too. In the end, after a big fight, I walked away. I found myself with a new group of friends who didn't really like me, but I didn't know the consequences of that decision at that time.

What followed was trauma. It planted seeds of fear, and one of the deepest was the fear of abandonment. I was terrified that everyone would eventually leave me. That fear kept me stuck. It made me stay in a toxic environment, holding on to friendships that weren't good for me, simply because I feared being alone.

I didn't feel lonely when I was by myself - I felt lonely when I was surrounded by people, pretending to fit in. In this group, I was always second, never the first priority. Everyone had their best friend, their go-to person. And I? I was just the one who tagged along. I often felt like an afterthought. They made sure I felt like a second priority. It sucked. But I stayed. Why? Because I was afraid of being left out. I tried to change myself-to adjust my likes, my dislikes - just to fit in. I bent over backward to please them, but no matter what I did, it was never enough. They didn't really like me, no matter what I did.

There were moments of happiness, yes, but they never lasted. The emotional toll was too heavy. Every birthday, every outing, every party, every trip,every gathering I was always the side character. My opinions? Never important. I was always judged, always criticized. And every time we fought, I was the one at fault. I was the one who had to fix things, to apologize, to make everything okay.

The years passed, and somewhere along the way, I lost myself. The need to please others, the desperate need for validation, created toxic behavior patterns in me, ones I didn't even realize were forming.

There was another fear I carried with me, one that I hadn't fully realized at the time. It was the fear of being vulnerable. The last time I had allowed myself to be vulnerable, it didn't end well. I had opened up, let my guard down, and exposed my heart, only to have it hurt, rejected, and disregarded. The pain from that experience lingered, and it taught me a lesson I didn't want to learn-that vulnerability could be dangerous.

So, I did what anyone would do to protcct themselves from that kind of pain. I built walls around my heart. Thick, impenetrable walls that no one could cross. I told myself it was better this way.

But as time passed, those walls became my shield, and I couldn't see how they were suffocating me. I became emotionally shut down. I withdrew from the world, not just from people who hurt me, but from everyone. It wasn't just about protecting myself anymore; I had stopped trusting my own feelings. I became unavailable-afraid to open up, afraid to feel.

The more I closed off, the more distant I became from everything and everyone around me. It wasn't that I didn't want to care. It wasn't that I didn't want to connect. I just couldn't. The walls I had built were too high, too thick. They kept the pain out, but they also kept the love out.

I became numb, and the emotional toll of that numbness began to weigh on me in ways I couldn't even articulate. I had to find a way to heal, to tear down those walls but I didn't know how to let myself be vulnerable again.

Some friends tried to reach out, tried to show me they cared, but it wasn't enough. It never was enough. Because in the end, I didn't know how to care for myself.

This emotional rock bottom didn't leave me much room to b e myself-to be that curious, energetic, happy person I once was. My confidence shattered, piece by piece, until there was nothing left but the hollow shell of who I used to be.

I had become accustomed to not taking any action, to not learning new skills, to just…existing. I felt numb. Every day was a struggle, but I smiled. I smiled because I didn't want anyone to see my pain, to pity me. The walls I had built around my heart were reinforced by this mask of happiness I wore for the world.

But despite everything, I still tried. I tried hard to study, to keep my head above water. I scored first class in all my years, and yet, deep down, I knew I was capable of more. So much more.

That realization left me with a deep sense of regret-an ache that wouldn't go away. I had the potential, the abilities, but I had never fully tapped into them. I had settled for mediocrity, for surviving rather than thriving. And that regret - that constant reminder that I hadn't reached my true potential—it stayed with me.

One day I woke up, I said to myself…NO MORE!!!! NO F**KING MORE!!!!

I had reached a breaking point. Enough was enough. I was tired of being trapped in my own fears, my own insecurities, and the numbness that had consumed me for so long. It was time to take control of my life again.

And so, I did.

I started by shifting my luggage to a new room-literally and metaphorically. A new room, a new life. The fear of being alone gripped me like never before, but I whispered to myself, "It's better to be alone than to keep living this miserable existence."

The day I moved, I cried like never before. The tears flowed endlessly, but for the first time, there was peace in those tears. It felt like I was shedding old skin. At that moment, I felt free. I felt happy. I felt calm. My heart was at peace. No more lingering insecurities, no more fears controlling my every move. I had liberated myself. I felt like I was born again.

So lesson here, your life will change on the day you start taking responsibility for it. And from that day on, I began doing all the things I had always wanted to do but never had the courage to.

Learn how to drive a scooty? - Check.

Buy a scooty? - Check.

Paint my wall with colors that made me feel alive? - Check.

Learn to drive a car? - Check.

Be the organizer in an event? - Check.

Walk like I own the world? - Check.

Wear dresses like I'm the prettiest? - Check.

So the lesson here, if you want to change your life, start by changing your environment.

As I started embracing this new chapter of my life, something beautiful happened-new friendships began to form. And some of the old ones, the ones that had weathered storms with me, grew even deeper. It was as though the walls I had built not only came down for me, but for others too. I became open to authentic connections, and the people who truly understood me started to show up. These friendships were no longer about fitting in or proving my worth. They were about mutual respect, trust, and genuine care.

I've come to realize just how lucky I am to have these people in my life. Some were new faces who showed up at just the right moment, while others were those who had been with me through the highs and lows, and now, our bond felt even stronger. I am truly grateful for these friendships. They've become my anchors, my support system, and my reminder that not everyone will leave.

Jealousy

There was a girl in my class. You know the kind—smart, wealthy, effortlessly cool, talented, the role model for everyone. Everyone adored her as a student, whether they realised it or not. And there I sat, calmly observing her from the rear. She and I appeared to be a perfect match because we had similar personalities and were both capable and ambitious. The difference is that I was at my own emotional lowest point and she acted while I did not. I decided not to paint the wall as I had intended. Later, when I got to her room, She had. I later learnt that she had done many of the things I had hoped to accomplish.

I was frequently taken aback by how similar our opinions and preferences could be. She embodied all of my dreams. She served as a continual reminder that I was becoming less of the inquisitive, driven person I once was. I certainly attempted to dislike her and looked for flaws in her to justify my lack of action, but one day I realised how hard I was trying to hate her. I became conscious of the thinking processes that resulted from my jealousy. I dreaded feeling jealous.

There was a faint bitterness in my heart that I had never experienced before. I wasn't really proud of it. I faced myself. I didn't enjoy feeling jealous, but the problem with jealousy is that it consumes you from the inside out, making you feel inadequate in some way. I became less aware of my own strengths the more I concentrated on hers. I therefore made the decision to reverse the situation. I began to look up to her as a role model and inspiration.

What would she do, I asked myself each time I failed. And the response was obvious. She'd do something and try again. The spark I lost somewhere along the line was rekindled by her. The lesson here is straightforward: Recognise that when someone is criticising or judging you, it is more about their own feelings of inadequacy and inadequacies than it is about you.

I no longer get offended when I see someone criticising me. In fact, I feel sorry for them since, unlike me, they haven't resolved their flaws yet.

Being born with flaws is okay. But dying with them? That's Not.

Feeling jealous is okay, but letting it consume you? That's where you draw the line.

WHITE COATS, DARK CIRCLES

— Dr. S. Sreeja, MBBS,
SVIMS- Sri Padmavathi Medical College for Women, Tirupati, AP, India.

"You don't have to be great to start, but you have to start to be great"

— *Zig Ziglar*

17

WHITE COATS, DARK CIRCLES

— Dr. S. Sreeja, MBBS,
SVIMS- Sri Padmavathi Medical College for Women, Tirupati, AP, India.

Exam Pressures: The Chaos and Grind

Like everyone else, I didn't study every day for the exams. When the time came, I'd grab my books, often too late, with exams just around the corner. And so began the grind-the last-minute cram sessions.

That was when the real work started: endless night outs surrounded by books,notes, and equally stressed friends. We'd study together, hoping to cover the syllabus but knowing, deep down, that there was no way we'd finish it all. What was greater-the pressure or the syllabus? Honestly, I couldn't tell. Both felt endless.

I remember those last-min lectures from friends—everyone scrambling to explain concepts that we all should have mastered weeks ago. And somehow, the anxiety wasn't only about what we had to study, but also about the little things that became big rituals: borrowing pens and erasers before entering the exam hall, praying to God before the exam began, hoping that somehow the universe would smile on us and grant us a passing grade.

Then came the exam itself. The stress of sitting in that room, flipping through pages only to realize we had forgotten everything we'd studied. The worst part was not even remembering simple facts when the pressure hit. As I scribbled down answers, I could feel the panic rise —did I even know the right answer? And sometimes, when the truth hit, I'd realize I had written something entirely wrong. That was always a moment of sinking dread, hoping somehow that the examiner wouldn't notice, or that the passing mark was a bit more forgiving.

And yet, we'd still find humor in it. After the exam, we'd gather in groups and laugh about t h e absurd answers we gave, joking about how our exams must've looked like complete nonsense. It was our way of coping with the fear and exhaustion.

The final relief came after the exam—the overwhelming feeling of peace as soon as the papers were submitted. All the tension would melt away. Even if I had no idea how I did, that moment of completion was worth every ounce of stress leading up to it. It felt like a temporary reprieve, like I was finally free from the storm, even if just for a moment. then I would get the best sleep of my life.

Imposter Syndrome

I thought I was prepared for medical school. I had dreams, ambitions, and a burning desire to make a difference. But no one told me about the voice in my head that would constantly question my worth. It wasn't something anyone warned me about. In fact, no one talks about it openly, but imposter syndrome—the feeling of being a fraud, of not truly deserving the title you've worked so hard to earn-quietly crept into my life.

There I was, surrounded by brilliant minds, classmates who seemed to know it all, and professors who carried an air of authority and expertise. And then there was me. I couldn't shake the thought that I was somehow less than them, that I didn't belong in the same room, that my achievements were just a stroke of luck.

Every time I received praise or recognition, a part of me wondered if it was a mistake, if I was merely pretending to be capable, and eventually, everyone would see through me. The success I had worked for and thought I deserved felt like it had been handed to me without merit. I started doubting my skills, my knowledge, and even my passion for medicine. My confidence was shattered with every mistake or failure. It felt like every time I made a misstep, I was confirming the truth: that I was never meant to be here.

But the truth is, imposter syndrome is a universal feeling. In medical school, it's easy to feel like you're constantly under a microscope. The stakes are high, the pressure is intense, and the expectations are overwhelming. You're asked to carry the weight of life in your hands, but in the back of your mind, you're questioning whether you're even worthy of being there.

There were days when I thought, Why me? Why was I chosen to be a doctor? There were others more capable, more knowledgeable, more deserving. Yet, every day, I kept showing up, pushing through the self-doubt, even when I felt like I was faking my way through the system.

But somewhere along the way, I realized that imposter syndrome doesn't define me. It's not about being perfect or never making mistakes; it's about continuing to grow, to learn, and to push forward despite self-doubt. Every surgeon, every doctor I admired once had their own struggles, their own fears, their own moments of uncertainty. They are not immune to imposter syndrome either. What sets them apart is their ability to face it, acknowledge it, and rise above it.

So I'm learning to embrace the discomfort. I remind myself that I'm here because I worked for it. I may not have all the answers, but that's okay. I am constantly learning, evolving, and becoming a better version of myself. In a profession that demands perfection, I am giving myself permission to not always be perfect. After all, medicine is not just about the knowledge-it's about the heart, the resilience, and the willingness to grow.

And maybe, just maybe, I'm not an imposter after all.

Internship: Finding peace in chaos

During my internship, I found a strange sense of peace in the chaos of medicine. As eager as I was to learn and grow, I discovered something unexpected: the act of working became a sort of meditation for me. When I focused on the tasks at hand, everything else-my fears, insecurities, overthinking-melted away. It was as if I was transported to a place where only the work mattered. I didn't have to worry about anything else. It was peaceful, and it allowed me to clear my mind in ways nothing else could.

When I started in the medicine department, I never really felt the overwhelming pressure that most people associate with the responsibility of holding lives in your hands. Even when the situation was dire, even when someone's life hung in the balance, I didn't panic. I don't know if that's a good thing or a bad thing, but I remained calm-almost detached in a way. Maybe it was my inexperience or my way of coping, but I never felt that stress or fear that I expected to feel.

One particular night, during my night duty at a small, remote hospital-one that rarely saw patients-everything changed. We had an odd case, and for once, it wasn't a slow night. A man came in, sweating and complaining of pain in his left shoulder. I suspected myocardial infarction. Without hesitation, I instructed the nurse to do an ECG. But things quickly took a turn. The patient collapsed.

I started CPR, doing everything I could in the moment. The problem was, there was no defibrillator available and very few resources to continue proper treatment. With nothing but my training and instincts guiding me, I felt a faint pulse, and I immediately sent him to a specialty hospital for further care. Unfortunately, the patient didn't make it. I felt sadness wash over me, but surprisingly, I wasn't terrified. I was caught off guard, yes, but I dealt with the situation as best I could.

That experience became a turning point for me. I realized that, deep down, I could be a great doctor if I truly put in the effort. But more than that, I also realized how much I loved the emergency situations. The adrenaline, the intensity-it didn't scare me; it invigorated me. I felt alive in those moments.

But a part of me also knew something else. At that moment, I wasn't fully responsible for the patient's life; I was still just an intern. Maybe that's what allowed me to maintain my calm in the chaos. I was still learning, still under the protective wing of my seniors. I wasn't carrying the weight of someone's life on my shoulders entirely.

But despite that, I knew one thing for sure: I loved being a doctor. And it wasn't just about the moments of life-saving; it was about being in the midst of it all and learning how to navigate the chaos with a steady hand. I was ready to grow, to take on more, to truly make a difference.

The Surgical Dream: From Grey's Anatomy to Reality

My journey took me to the surgical department, and as soon as I stepped in, I knew I was where I belonged. It all started with a simple TV show-Grey's Anatomy. It wasn't just a show for me; it was a revelation. Watching those surgeons work, the precision, the grace under pressure-it sparked something deep inside me. The idea of surgery, of being able to heal through the power of your hands, was something that captivated me. Was it the satisfaction of saving a life? Was it the artistry of suturing, or perhaps the bloodied hands that symbolized a job well done? I don't know. But it felt like magic, and for the first time, I felt like I had found my true calling.

In the operating room, I felt invincible, like a superhero. The surgical gown and gloves were my cape, and with every incision, I imagined myself making a difference in someone's life. The technique of suturing, the careful precision of each stitch-it was all so fascinating. The moment I made that first cut, I felt an adrenaline rush like no other.

But there was a catch. I was too lean and weak to handle the physical demands of surgery. Some days, I could stand for seven hours straight, lost in the rhythm of the operation. Other days, I'd feel dizzy after just an hour, my body protesting against the physical strain. It was a strange disconnect- my mind was eager, but my body wasn't always on the same page. I couldn't understand why my body worked the way it did, and I struggled with this constant battle between my passion and my physical limitations.

Yet, despite these challenges, I'm here today, taking up General Surgery as my postgraduate course. I don't know how I'll overcome the fatigue and physical exhaustion that comes with long surgeries, but I'm confident of one thing: I can do anything I set my heart to. The road ahead may be tough, and I might face moments of doubt, but I know that passion and determination are stronger than any physical obstacle. I will push through.

This is my dream, and I'll fight for it with everything I have.

THE EBBS AND FLOWS: A JOURNEY THROUGH UNCERTAINTY

— Dr. Sujani Raja, MBBS,
SVIMS- Sri Padmavathi Medical College for Women, Tirupati, AP, India.

*"Life will bring you pain all by itself, Your responsibility
is to create joy"*

— Milton Erickson

18

THE EBBS AND FLOWS: A JOURNEY THROUGH UNCERTAINTY

— Dr. Sujani Raja, MBBS,
SVIMS- Sri Padmavathi Medical College for Women, Tirupati, AP, India.

Stepping out of the bubble

The real world begins when you step out of your medical college, when you leave that bubble protected by your professors and seniors, the path you wanted to take sets up your next hurdles not an easy one though, either you decide to work or pursue higher studies nothing becomes easier. you get to know your ways of life hard! The expectations, the realizations, the hardships, the blessings, the experiences that make THE WHOLE YOU.

The hopes

The first phase of becoming you, you may call it 'The prep phase' of course the NEET PG, the OG path to follow after MBBS where you can find most of the medicos trying to find their mode of transportation (which platform of preparation), their destinations(which branch), their life time travel partners(well you know!), and almost everyone questioning everything through the whole journey. At the end you may see people reaching their destinations they desired and few reaching their destinations that are destined and few still traveling. One might be lying if they say that this path seems fine and furnished compared to others, only NEET PG 2024 aspirants know how fine it was as I was saying nothing becomes easier.

The challenges of adulthood

Navigating adulthood is tough enough, but the demands of being a doctor makes it even more daunting, as we grow up we get responsibilities of taking care of our family as health is major portion that controls every family dynamics guess how demanding and daunting it is to be a first generation doctor, to make it even more daunting mbbs graduate becomes just mbbs graduate.

Initially everything seems fine and of course eventually everything will get better at the end probably once you start your practice or maybe in the long run. The initial days seems fun even though it is scary, don't we all love watching a horror film or try a scary ride I know the comparison looks a bit ridiculous but that's one of the things I learned from adulting, using humor to brush off things and yeah it is a proven mature defence mechanism scientifically. Why I call this a fun is being in medical field already proves that they were all enthusiasts once and gathering more knowledge, more Learning, new environment, the enthusiasm of entering next phase of life, arranging your daily routines, adding new routines, the trail and errors of learning, living, loving the version you are becoming, the expectation and hope for best destination is per se fun and amazing. The hope and expectation of reaching the best destination make the journey exciting.

A never ending cycle

Even though having an undeniable enthusiasm to learn, we tend to forget often and the learning never ends here. We keep learning things and forgetting them eventually and end up feeling bad for doing so either skipping the question in exam or failing in viva which is acceptable but being in medical field such incidents may cost more but if you get a chance to relearn everything but this time you know the seriousness of being a medico and topics you found either hard to understand or not that easy to retain in our memory happens to understand better makes you amazed.

The amount of happiness, relief we get becomes unexplainable. Some might wonder, isn't it the primary responsibility in MBBS to learn them in the first place? It may sound unacceptable but weren't we all kids at some point in our lives? Taking things less serious, being an average student I spent my ug days scared and afraid, I didn't get a moment to cherish that I'm studying a subject that saves lives, fear was the only companion I got throughout my whole UG, I did got some moments to cherish as when my family is having an occasion at home, I performed my first amputation, when whole world is sleeping, I assisted a birth of a baby these may seem like regular duties but I implore you to understand that they hold a great value to someone who feared everything and instead of cherishing them I feared them.

Realising the beauty of medicine

This is when I realized the beauty of medicine, the minute things that happen in the human body, the intricate mechanisms. The prep phase has given me those reminders to cherish the privilege of studying medicine, to celebrate the wonders of the body and how it works, to love and enjoy the joy of learning instead of fear. Even though I had fear all along the way, it made me feel it in a rational way. One such class is medicine where we were learning about covid even though covid held a major role in changing our lives we took that topic to ease to learn as it is not in the curriculum, we have known the screening methods, treatment protocols but never understood the concept behind those things neither did I try to learn in my ug nor did it even cross my mind to do so.

Moments that Inspired

Another such class where I felt amazed for all those small, tiny but important things that existed in the universe and their discoveries. As a science group student, most of us hated physics and I had thought what's the need of learning it to become a doctor, but let alone becoming a doctor you need physics and its application everyday and every second for our whole existence. So the class was physiology > cardiovascular system > haemodynamics where we were taught about the physics that is happening in our body, how atheroma can dislodge and aneurysm can rupture using bernoulli's law, how untreated hypertension can lead to left ventricular hypertrophy using Laplace law ultimately which may lead to heart failure, arrhythmia, MI and sudden cardiac death. Here the things that awestruck me were the clinical application of these principles, the kinetic and potential energies, the tension relating to wall thickness and radius of blood vessel these factors being altered by a disease condition and how they alter the presentation of the case made me feel how amazing is the human body! How amazing is the creation! how amazing it is that everything is interlinked! That moment made me feel how grateful we are to be in a place to understand the magic of the creator and his creation.

The Overthinking

This profession just doesn't make you proud and happy. It comes with much more like fear, regrets, anxiety, stress, confusion, sacrifices, self doubts, embarrassment and guilt. Looking back to when I was an extrovert, I often wonder how I became an introvert and afraid of the unknown. This preparation phase has made me realise that I'm afraid of what future is holding, what if I'm not competent enough, what if I fail in what I'm doing now, what if I don't get to do my post graduation, what if I don't get into the branch I wanted to, what if I get into branch I hate, what if i end up hating the branch that I like, or what if I want to quit then! Will my people agree to that? Will they support me? These thoughts may occur to most of us and we overcome some of them but my concern here is how much of these thoughts can we manage to be a sane person. The irony here being medicos we know what is acceptable and what is not yet we just let our overthinking take charge sometimes.

The Inner Battle: Head vs Heart

This overthinking once got me questioning my whole existence and the way of life I wanted to live. The whole time I have been trying to decide how to live, I know everything we do is for the survival, the effort and hardworking in this labyrinth of existence some of us never stumble upon the sacred hourglass of joy, few forget to be happy, few forget to laugh, few forget to live. The internship period had taught me so much that it made my mind and heart combat between the way of living the life I chose and the life I might want. I read this in a book where the author goes as 'The head and heart must forge a lifetime partnership if one wants to live a beautiful life, live completely in the head and you can't feel the breath and rhythm of life, live completely in the heart and you may find yourself acting like a lovestruck fool, with poor judgement and no discipline'. I guess we all can relate to this pretty much in almost most of the situations in our daily life. In my situation I don't mean that I don't want to be in this profession but the realization it gave about life and death made me question why must I leave my life behind hardworking, leaving behind peace and happiness. The deaths I have seen and the situations the people died and the constant despair that people and loved ones gives by sharing only their sorrows and health issues further makes me feel sick about life, to a point where I started questioning the whole existence of humans and this question sparked a yearning to live a life to fullest.

The Everlasting Struggle

The decision to prioritize happiness and authenticity often demands sacrifice and forces us to reconsider the paths we have walked so far. I too did some rethinking of my past decisions, I am not that kind of person who regrets past decisions based on present outcome as I strongly believe in destiny, if it is meant to happen, it will have a reason behind it, we may not feel good about it or not benefited immediately but the universe definitely have a reason for it. The incidents that happened in my life made me realise this, one such incident is the whole reason for where I stand now. But the constant worry you get when things are not going well, when self doubt creeps in, when things once looked fine but now just seems to fall apart even though you know everything will fall in right place you just can't get away from it how much ever optimistic you are, how much ever you believe in destiny, you have to continue with what you are doing right now. That's one of the lessons I learnt in this phase. You have to deal with whatever you are going through physically, mentally you have to do the role for the day that is studying. People will also tell you to take some time for yourselves but it's easier said than done, you can't do it without the guilt of not studying for the day, without the fomo, without planning the upcoming schedule. The time for yourself will still be occupied by thoughts ' I didn't complete my schedule yesterday, I didn't get the target score in last grand test, I did a silly mistake in answering that question', here again your heart wants to do something and your head wants to do something else.ultimately you will learn to prioritize things you will take care of our health both physical and mental.

Building Resilience

The daily routines you do to keep you healthy and sane comes handy during breakdowns, the yoga, exercises, meditation, prayers will definitely help, they may not provide you with solutions for the current problem but they provide you with strength and resilience, the ability to withstand,recover and adapt in the face of adversities. They don't make you immune to difficulties or setbacks, but rather make you able to navigate through challenges and helps getting coping skills, positive outlooks and flexibility.

A Bittersweet Tale

Speaking of priority, you might think of things we had lost just because we were concentrating on something else that is important at the moment. The lost friendships, the relationships, the family events, the bonds, the sense of self. We console ourselves saying the outcomes will be beautiful but the flip side of the coin is loss, the loss of our beloved bonds, the loss of our youth, sitting at a study table. The bond that ends without our knowledge is kind of pathetic, you can't blame yourselves or the other person as the mistake is of the destiny. But the beauty of such bonds is they pick up where they had left. How much ever we feel sorry for breaking up such bonds, we need that breakups to move forward in life, to start the next phase of life, I'm not talking about the love kind of bonds they are supposed to be there for us always no matter what the situation demands, the friendships that break take us to next part,may be we are supposed to travel only that far with them but the beauty lies in how we cherish those bonds, them and their memories, the moments they were being there for us. For those friendships and bonds, like petals bloom and softly fade, leaving the traces of laughter and moments that won't evade. Those bonds that just expect happiness and success for you. The once in a while phone calls covering the whole life we missed together, the once in a while may be in months or years meet up bringing back the old fun vibes are enough to carry forward. My only request for such lost bonds is when someone remembers and makes an effort to call us, instead of blame or guilt tripping them for not reaching us before or for being busy, appreciate the effort they took to make a call or text. And there are some friends who stays with and helps with everything we go through, the unpaid therapists, the personal counselors, the partners in crime, the long distanced ones or the stuck with you ones, these bonds neither let you feel that you are the only one that sucks in life nor let you down no matter what. They form the pillars bearing your mental breakdowns. The only thing we need is a coffee break, a small ride with them to make our day brighter, it's not the coffee or roaming that brings peace its the person, a heartfelt conversation or just random dumping of our thoughts with them. They are doing this, we listen and we don't judge trends for a while. They are the ones who validate you even when you have self doubts.

The Need for Validation

Don't we all need validation for things we feel or things we do, let alone others even from ourselves. The situations we go through and the emotions we feel makes us what we are now and will continue to mould us, the appreciation we get for our achievements, the appreciation we get just for existing in someone's life, the anger and hatred for our mistakes, the embarrassment for being ignorant or momentarily foolish, the resentments for disappointing others, the body shamings, the gender discrimination, the judgements for the profession. The major role was played and is being played by the last things in almost everyone's life being said that body Shaming and gender discrimination makes us feel bad for matters that are not our choice, making our childhood disturbing and the judgements for being doctor makes our adulthood difficult, at least that we now know how to ignore unwanted things, we ourselves struggle to get to this place fighting of many things within ourselves, the creeping self doubt,the hopelessness, the mental breakdowns, adding the societal judgements and peer pressure makes it even hard to stand. The preparation phase is one where a graduate decides to study further leaving behind everything it may be their decision in the first place for getting into a desired branch but every other's opinion gets in that way of their decision.

The Detrimental Impact

While preparation either with joy or with hate the only wish everyone will have is to get into a better place, the news we daily see and hear in news that doctors getting attacked,attempting suicides is not very encouraging to the pg aspirants it makes us fear for the job, it makes us fear for life. I'm neither supporting wrong treatments nor supporting leaving alone the people who do that, the point is the one who studies these many years wishes to save or atleast makes lives better, doesn't want to end someone's life intentionally. There are laws and courts, let them decide, one thing we all learn growing up is no violence but we don't follow that when we grow up! These things do have an impact on fellow doctors who are growing up and budding ug aspirants who are wishing to join MBBS. People praise doctors for their service, call them God and beat the shit out of them. Being in the medical field we have seen both sides of stories as a health care provider and also as a patient's attender and as patients as well so I can assure that almost all of us have empathy towards patients.

The Lesson of Patience

However even within our households, parents may not follow what we say sometimes and it can be infuriating sometimes, the lesson to be patient when dealing with people starts within your own household. The patience to wait for something to happen is the ultimate test one can take and neet pg 2024 is one such test itself, the twists and turns draining the little positivity I had, to a point where I can no longer process the emotions and react the way it's supposed to be! And the result was not promising, not even satisfactory where I had to take another dropout.

The Pressure of Overachievement

We being overachievers linking our personal life with the things we achieve professionally. And I'm not an exception to this. It took me months to get back together myself. The regret and questions that you get in mind when you are stuck at someplace is really horrible. The feeling when you look back where you had fun, stood up for yourself, had a long break, took some rest, did light work sometimes, thinking I have got this, I can do this but end up not getting what you wanted in spite of hard work is something unexplainable. The self blame, the self doubt of haven't I concentrated properly? Haven't I did put my whole effort? Haven't I put enough of myself into this? Am I not worth it? why should it have a goal-sacrifice everything else. Why can't you work right, you are having fun, you are taking some rest and you get what you want. Maybe if I had got what I wanted, would I have appreciated myself for sacrificing those? or would I have regretted not being easy on myself?

The Impact of Anxiety

The major thing that made me question my whole way of seeing goal oriented life and natural, fun, peace loving way of living is my anxiety, every time I get anxious I'm nauseous that made me afraid of food and to eat to a point where I thought I might want to get therapy for my anxiety. That's when I learnt to put my overthinking in the backseat and let living in the present takeover, one thing at a moment, taking one step at a time. The biggest lesson life teaches is you are your own supporter and biggest cheerleader when no one understands you. You go through a lot whatever thing that had happened small or big, it takes away a part of us, our happiness, our joy, where we just try to be alive and do what we are supposed to do and feel those humanly feelings grief, anger, stress where we don't want to talk to anybody about anything, then after sometime you feel better you wanted someone to talk about things but you are left with none no one who can help you, understand you by the time you try to open up everyone will be moved on to the next thing in their life or drowning with their own problems everytime we campaign in books, social media that we should be there to talk to people who are struggling but what if that struggling person is unable (not unwilling) to even utter a word about what they are going through? So being there for ourselves, even if we failed to achieve something or being miserable at something we should go easy on ourselves and try again if we want to do that so badly. You need courage to walk through your fear in pursuit of a goal and here I am getting my courage back.

FINDING HOME AWAY FROM HOME: MY CARIBBEAN MEDICAL SCHOOL EXPERIENCE

— *Dr. Shrishti P. Khetan, MD, MHA,*
American University of Barbados, Wildey, Saint Michael, Barbados.

*"Every great move forward in your life begins with a leap of faith,
a step into the unknown."*

— Brian Tracy

19

FINDING HOME AWAY FROM HOME: MY CARIBBEAN MEDICAL SCHOOL EXPERIENCE

— Dr. Shrishti P. Khetan, MD, MHA,
American University of Barbados, Wildey, Saint Michael, Barbados.

Farewell to Familiar Streets

Thinking back, there were so many emotions swirling in my mind when I decided to attend medical school in Barbados. It felt like I was being pulled into a whirlwind. As a girl from Mumbai, leaving behind everything familiar—the bustling streets filled with the aroma of street food, the comfort of home-cooked meals—was a big adjustment. But the allure of pursuing my dream of becoming a doctor amidst turquoise waters and sandy beaches was too enthralling to resist.

I knew life as a medical student wouldn't be the island paradise often pictured on postcards. One only truly understands the challenge that lies beyond those breathtaking landscapes when they take on the rigorous academics of medical school.

In this chapter, I document how I adapted, grew, and exchanged cultures while navigating the vibrant colors, sounds, and rhythms of life in Barbados. Ultimately, I found something unexpected—a home away from home.

A Warm Welcome

Grantley Adams International Airport greeted me with a rush of warm, tropical air and a sea of unfamiliar accents. Coming from Mumbai, where the air is thick with pollution and traffic noise, the island's laid-back pace felt both soothing and disorienting. The lush green hills and endless stretches of beaches screamed paradise, but beneath that beauty lay the challenge of carving out a place for myself in this new world.

Adjusting to Island Rhythms

As a vegetarian, adapting to the local cuisine was a puzzle. I deeply missed pani puri, pav bhaji, and all the flavors of home. However, I discovered fantastic alternatives like rice and peas, breadfruit, and plantain. Experimenting with local ingredients allowed me to blend my Indian roots with Barbadian flavors—a metaphor for my journey of finding harmony in contrast.

The warmth of the people was another unexpected comfort. The Bajans, with their easy smiles and welcoming nature, made me feel like I belonged. Many of my fellow students were also away from home, and together, we formed a patchwork family—eating, studying, and struggling through the demands of medical school side by side.

These friendships and the kindness of the locals became my anchors, keeping me grounded in the whirlwind of medical school.

A Global Classroom: Diverse Perspectives

One of the most enriching aspects of my experience was the cultural diversity in our classroom. My classmates came from different corners of the world, each bringing unique perspectives to our discussions. A student from Canada would share insights about their healthcare system, while a classmate from the Caribbean would offer perspectives shaped by small island communities.

These exchanges reinforced the universality of medicine. Despite our diverse backgrounds, we shared a common goal—to heal and make a difference. Discussing different global healthcare systems not only broadened my understanding but also made me more empathetic as a future physician.

Patient Care Across Cultures

During clinical rotations, cultural understanding became an invaluable skill. Patients had different beliefs about health and healing, and learning to navigate these differences was crucial.

For instance, I encountered patients who preferred traditional remedies over modern medicine. Instead of dismissing their beliefs, I learned to build trust and find ways to integrate their perspectives into effective care. This experience reinforced the idea that medicine is not just about science—it's about understanding people, their fears, and their hopes.

Island Adventures

Barbados wasn't just my classroom—it was my playground. I embraced the island's culture, attending Crop Over festivals, exploring hidden coves, and indulging in the rhythm of calypso music. I tasted exotic fruits like sugar apples and found solace in the breathtaking beauty of Crane Beach.

Homesickness & Resilience

Despite the adventures, homesickness hit hard—especially during festivals like Diwali. I longed for the glow of diyas, the scent of sweets, and the warmth of family gatherings.

But those moments of longing strengthened my resilience. Instead of dwelling on what I missed, I started creating my own little celebrations, introducing my classmates to Indian traditions while immersing myself in theirs. Over time, these shared experiences built a deeper sense of connection.

Learning, Growing, and Becoming

My time in Barbados wasn't just about academics; it was a journey of self-discovery. Growing up in Mumbai, life was always fast-paced, every moment accounted for. The island taught me to slow down, to live in the present, and to appreciate the beauty of simple moments.

Being in a culturally diverse environment pushed me beyond my comfort zone. I learned that our borders don't define our compassion. Medicine became more than a profession—it became a way to connect with people from all walks of life.

Lessons from an Island Journey

As I reflect on my Caribbean medical school experience, I see a journey of growth, resilience, and—most importantly—connection. I was once a nervous girl boarding a flight to an unknown land. But I became someone who found a second home in a distant corner of the world.

To anyone considering studying abroad, I would say: embrace the unfamiliar. Step outside your comfort zone—that's where the greatest lessons are learned. My time in Barbados taught me that home is not just a place. It is a feeling, a connection, and a state of mind.

THE DIFFERENCE IN MEDICAL EDUCATION STYLES: FROM THE CARIBBEAN TO THE U.S

— *Dr. Shrishti P. Khetan, MD, MHA,*
American University of Barbados, Wildey, Saint Michael, Barbados.

"Success is not final, failure is not fatal: it is the courage to continue that counts."

— Winston Churchill

20

THE DIFFERENCE IN MEDICAL EDUCATION STYLES: FROM THE CARIBBEAN TO THE U.S

— *Dr. Shrishti P. Khetan, MD, MHA,*
American University of Barbados, Wildey, Saint Michael, Barbados.

A Journey from the Caribbean to U.S. Clinical Rotations

Medical education is not a one-size-fits-all model. My journey—from completing pre med and an MD in the Caribbean to clinical rotations in the U.S.—exposed me to two distinct educational frameworks. The Caribbean model, with its interactive and community-centered approach, and the fast-paced, patient-focused clinical environment in the U.S. each played a crucial role in shaping me as a medical professional. This chapter explores how early clinical exposure, research opportunities, and community engagement in the Caribbean provided a solid foundation for navigating the challenges of modern medicine.

Laying the Groundwork: Pre Med in Barbados

Reflecting on my early entry into pre med, I appreciate the dynamic approach to foundational sciences in Barbados. Over four semesters, I experienced an education system that emphasized interactive learning, where professors used case studies, group discussions, and presentations to simplify complex concepts.

One defining feature of this program was its strong focus on research and public speaking. From the first semester, we were encouraged to analyze case studies and present findings, which nurtured both confidence and analytical thinking. Additionally, mock interviews prepared us for future clinical roles by instilling professionalism and effective communication skills.

The MD Program: Merging Clinical Exposure with Research

The transition to the MD program was marked by a stronger clinical and community orientation. Unlike the Indian system, where patient exposure is often delayed, the Caribbean model introduced hands-on clinical engagement from the outset. Alongside lectures in anatomy, pathology, and pharmacology, we conducted physical examinations, participated in hospital rounds, and learned to interpret diagnostic tests.

Research and innovation were also key aspects of our training. We were taught to critically evaluate medical literature and develop evidence-based solutions for patient care. One of my most memorable projects involved researching the impact of lifestyle interventions on Type 2 diabetes management. This experience not only strengthened my research skills but also reinforced the importance of preventive medicine and teamwork.

Beyond the Classroom: Community Engagement and Practical Training

The Caribbean medical education system emphasized interactive teaching methods and holistic learning. Case-based discussions and simulation labs were integral to our training, allowing us to practice CPR, suturing, intubation, and other essential procedures on high-fidelity mannequins. These hands-on experiences built my confidence and prepared me for real-world clinical challenges.

Beyond academics, our curriculum prioritized community outreach and cultural awareness. We participated in health camps, conducted blood pressure screenings, educated communities about diabetes management, and advocated for vaccination programs. Events like the annual Breast Cancer Awareness Walk provided valuable opportunities to engage with patients and promote early detection and prevention.

Cultural events further enriched our education. International food fairs and student-led initiatives fostered camaraderie among peers from diverse backgrounds. These experiences enhanced my cultural competence—a skill that proved invaluable during my clinical rotations in Chicago.

A Tale of Two Systems: Comparing Caribbean and Indian Medical Education

The Caribbean and Indian medical education systems differ significantly in their approach. The Indian model leans heavily on theoretical knowledge in the early years, ensuring a solid conceptual foundation before clinical application. In contrast, the Caribbean curriculum balances theory with practical exposure from the beginning.

For instance, while I conducted patient interviews and presented case histories under the guidance of experienced physicians, my peers in India spent their first two years primarily immersed in textbooks. This early clinical exposure helped me develop patient-centered care skills and critical thinking abilities.

That said, the Indian system's strong emphasis on theoretical depth is also valuable. Observing my Indian peers' extensive knowledge base motivated me to strike a balance between theoretical understanding and practical application.

U.S. Clinical Rotations: Applying Global Learning to Patient Care

My experiences in Barbados equipped me with a strong foundation for clinical rotations in the U.S. The hands-on training, emphasis on self-learning, and exposure to community health prepared me to thrive in a diverse and fast-paced healthcare environment like Chicago.

During rotations, I noticed that my Caribbean education gave me a unique edge. I was confident in taking patient histories, conducting physical exams, and presenting cases. My research background also allowed me to engage in evidence-based discussions with attending physicians.

Additionally, the mock interviews and presentation skills honed in Barbados proved invaluable. Whether explaining patient cases or discussing treatment plans with senior doctors, I was able to communicate clearly and professionally—a skill that significantly enhanced my clinical experience.

Integrating Global Perspectives in Medicine

My medical education in the Caribbean not only provided me with a rigorous academic foundation but also fostered community involvement, research skills, and cultural adaptability. The early clinical exposure, interactive teaching methods, and community engagement initiatives shaped me into a well-rounded, compassionate, and competent physician.

Both the Caribbean and Indian models offer valuable lessons. The Caribbean approach instilled confidence, flexibility, and a patient-centered perspective, while the Indian system reinforced the importance of in-depth theoretical knowledge. Together, these experiences have prepared me to navigate the ever-evolving world of medicine, bridging cultures and thriving in a global healthcare landscape.

CLINICAL ROTATIONS IN CHICAGO: CHALLENGES AND REWARDS

— *Dr. Shruti Suresh Suvarna, MD, MHA,*
American University of Barbados,Wildey, Saint Michael, Barbados.

"To that feeling, we are just getting started"

— *BTS*

21

CLINICAL ROTATIONS IN CHICAGO: CHALLENGES AND REWARDS

— Dr. Shruti Suresh Suvarna, MD, MHA,
American University of Barbados,Wildey, Saint Michael, Barbados.

Medically, it was humbling; professionally, it was exhilarating—navigating the maze of the U.S. healthcare system as a medical student from an international school. My clinical rotations in Chicago's South and West Sides, rich in the realities of American medicine, exposed me to a diverse patient population, a wide range of pathologies, and the challenges of limited resources and complex healthcare systems. These experiences largely defined my choice of specialty and my career path.

First Day Jitters

I remember the first day of every single one of my rotations. Standing outside the hospital entrance in my crisp white coat, badge in hand, I felt an overwhelming mix of excitement and nervousness. My heart pounded as I took in the towering hospital building, the flurry of healthcare workers rushing in and out, and the realization that I was about to step into a whole new world—one that I had dreamed of for so long.

As I walked in, my stomach twisted with anticipation. I was desperate to make a good impression, to prove that I belonged. The nervous energy was almost paralyzing, but at the same time, there was this electrifying thrill—this was it, the beginning of something incredible.

After being introduced to my team, I felt a momentary sense of relief. My fellow teammates, a mix of residents and medical students, were welcoming, but I knew I had to find my place among them. The hospital was a maze—hallways stretching endlessly, different units buzzing with activity, codes being called, and the constant hum of the EMRs. in the background. I had to figure out my ins and outs quickly—where to find my patients, where rounds would begin, and how to navigate the fast-paced rhythm of hospital life.

Despite the initial anxiety, every single moment felt amazing. The adrenaline of being in the middle of real patient care, the weight of responsibility, and the realization that I was finally living my dream—it was exhilarating. The challenge of keeping up, of learning, of proving to myself that I could handle this, made my heart race in the best way possible. I knew that from this moment on, I was exactly where I was meant to be.

Lessons from a Diverse Patient Population

Rotating through hospitals on the South and West Sides of Chicago meant encountering an incredibly diverse patient population. Each patient brought more than just a medical history; they carried a story shaped by their socioeconomic and cultural background. These experiences taught me that medicine doesn't always have a one-size-fits-all solution.

From gunshot wounds to uncontrolled diabetes, from advanced cancers to rare genetic disorders—I saw it all. One memorable case was a middle-aged woman in preeclampsia requiring an emergency C-section. Watching the team function seamlessly under pressure to save both mother and baby reinforced the importance of teamwork and communication in achieving effective patient care.

My First On-Call Night: A Defining Moment

I had no idea what to expect on my first on-call night during my OB-GYN rotation. The labor and delivery unit buzzed with anticipation. Around midnight, my attendant turned to me and said, "Shruti, get ready—you're helping with a delivery."

A rush of adrenaline surged through me. My mind raced with excitement, but nervousness settled in just as quickly. Was I ready for this? Could I handle the responsibility? There was no time to dwell on my doubts. I scrubbed in, my hands slightly trembling, my heart pounding in my chest. The delivery room was a symphony of controlled chaos—nurses preparing instruments, the attending giving sharp commands, and the mother pushing through waves of pain. I stood there, taking it all in, feeling like I was on the brink of something life-changing.

Then, in a moment that felt like it lasted forever, the baby arrived. A tiny, fragile life, crying and full of energy. I could barely breathe as the attendant turned to me and said, "You've earned it. Go ahead—cut the cord." I hesitated just for a second, my hands steady but my heart still racing. As I made the cut, a wave of emotions hit me—relief, triumph, and an overwhelming sense of awe. And then, the most incredible moment of all: I was handed the baby.

I held that newborn in my arms, feeling its warmth, hearing its cries, and realizing that I had just played a part in bringing a life into the world. A deep happiness spread through me—I had done it. It was more than just a milestone; it was a moment that solidified why I chose medicine. I wasn't just an observer in my journey anymore. I was a doctor in the making, and I knew with certainty that this was what I was meant to do.

Personal Growth and Key Takeaways

Each rotation had its challenges, but all had their rewards. I learned to think on my feet, communicate effectively with patients and their families, and remain calm in high-pressure situations. But beyond the clinical skills, these experiences shaped me in ways I never expected.

I remember the first time I had to deliver bad news to a patient's family—it was heartbreaking. No amount of medical knowledge could have prepared me for the raw emotions in that room. I felt their pain, their fear, and in that moment, I realized that medicine isn't just about diagnosing and treating—it's about being there for people when they need it the most.

There were days I felt completely exhausted, questioning if I was strong enough for this journey. But then there were moments—like when a patient smiled at me in gratitude or when a mentor reassured me that I was doing well—that reminded me why I started this path in the first place. Medicine has a way of humbling you, teaching you patience, and showing you the resilience of the human spirit. I didn't just grow as a future doctor; I grew as a person. And through it all, I realized that being a physician isn't just about treating diseases—it's about being present, listening, and making a difference, one patient at a time.

Advice for Aspiring Doctors

To aspiring doctors, especially international medical students, I offer this advice: embrace the journey with an open mind and a readiness to work hard. The road is tough, filled with moments of doubt and frustration, but the growth you experience is unparalleled.

I won't pretend it's easy. There were nights I lay awake, exhausted yet unable to sleep, replaying patient interactions in my mind—wondering if I had said the right thing, done enough, or if there was something I had missed. I've held the hands of patients who were terrified, seen families break down in despair, and experienced the helplessness of not always having the perfect answer. These moments stay with you, not as burdens, but as reminders of why you chose this path.

There is no textbook that can prepare you for the emotions that come with this profession. You will witness suffering, but you will also witness strength. You will see the worst days of people's lives, but you will also have the privilege of helping them through it. Medicine is not just about science; it is about humanity. It's about being there for someone, not just as a doctor, but as a source of comfort and hope.

So, to those stepping into this world, know that your struggles will shape you, your failures will teach you, and your empathy will define you. Be kind— to your patients, to your colleagues, and most importantly, to yourself. Because at the end of the day, being a doctor isn't just about saving lives—it's about touching them in a way that truly matters.

REFLECTION AND ADVICE FOR ASPIRING DOCTORS

— Dr. Shruti Suresh Suvarna, MD, MHA,
American University of Barbados,Wildey, Saint Michael, Barbados.

"The journey of a thousand miles begins with a single step."

— Lao Tzu

22

REFLECTION AND ADVICE FOR ASPIRING DOCTORS

— Dr. Shruti Suresh Suvarna, MD, MHA,
American University of Barbados, Wildey, Saint Michael, Barbados.

Looking Back on My Journey

My path to becoming a doctor was far from linear. Coming from a modest background in India, I took a less-traveled road—pursuing my medical degree in Barbados, followed by clinical rotations in Chicago. It was a journey filled with struggle and triumph, equally challenging and rewarding.

Adapting to a new educational system and culture was one of my biggest challenges. While the Caribbean environment was academically supportive, it also demanded a high level of self-discipline and adaptability. There were days when the weight of academic expectations and homesickness felt unbearable. However, these very challenges became catalysts for my personal and professional growth.

Triumphs came in many forms: excelling in clinical rotations and clerkships, interacting with grateful patients during my internal medicine clerkship, and gaining confidence in handling complex cases. These experiences reinforced the power of empathy and dedication in medicine.

Growth Through Struggles

Growing up in a sheltered home where everything was served on a platter, I had to learn to navigate life in even the smallest ways when I stepped out on my own. From managing daily chores to making crucial life decisions, every challenge pushed me to become more independent.

Being in a new country with no safety net taught me resilience. I learned to compartmentalize my priorities, set practical goals, and manage stress effectively. I built a strong network of friends who became my surrogate family, and each step reinforced my ability to stand strong on my own.

However, my journey wouldn't have been possible without the unwavering support of my family. They were my pillars of strength, cheering me on every step of the way. In moments of doubt and exhaustion, their belief in me uplifted my spirit. Their encouragement gave me the motivation to push through the hardest days, and for that, I am forever grateful.

This transformation shaped me into the woman I am today—resilient, independent, and unafraid to take on life's challenges. I eventually realized that success is not measured by how easily one attains their goals, but by how steadfastly one strives to achieve them.

Guidelines for Indian Students Contemplating International Medical Schools

1. **Research Thoroughly:** Before deciding, conduct thorough research. Check the school's accreditation, residency match rates, and available clinical rotations. Ensure the school aligns with your long-term goals—whether practicing in India, the U.S., or elsewhere.
2. **Financial Planning:** Studying abroad is a significant investment. Plan your finances carefully, explore scholarship opportunities, and budget for licensing exam costs like the USMLE.
3. **Prepare for Cultural Adaptation:** Moving to a new country means stepping out of your comfort zone. Embrace cultural differences but seek support when needed. Peers and mentors can help ease the transition.
4. **Master Time Management:** Balancing academics, clinical rotations, and personal well-being is crucial. Develop a structured study schedule while ensuring you take time for yourself.
5. **Stay Focused on Long-Term Goals:** Practicing medicine internationally is a long and challenging journey. Temporary setbacks should not cloud your vision. Each challenge is an opportunity for growth.

6. **Take Advantage of Clinical Rotations:** If your school offers clinical rotations in the U.S. or other countries, maximize the opportunity. These rotations provide invaluable exposure to different healthcare systems, enhance residency applications, and expand your professional network.

7. **Prioritize USMLE Preparation:** If you plan to practice in the U.S., start preparing for the USMLE early. Utilize question banks, review books, and online forums to structure your study plan.

8. **Build a Strong Support System:** Surround yourself with people who inspire and motivate you. Family, friends, and mentors can provide crucial support during the highs and lows of this journey.

Final Reflection

Looking back, my journey has been one of perseverance and adaptability. For aspiring doctors—especially from India—the path is undoubtedly tough, but it is worth every challenge. Each hurdle fosters growth, shaping you into a more compassionate, skilled, and resilient physician.

Choosing an international medical school may feel like stepping into the unknown, but courage and determination will guide you. Medicine is a lifelong journey, and every experience—both good and bad—adds to your story.

My Journey at a Glance

High School (12th Grade) → Pre-Med → Medical School ↳ Clinical Rotations (Chicago) → USMLE Step 1 → USMLE Step 2 ->OET -> ECFMG Certification ->Residency Preparation

UNITED STATES MEDICAL LICENSING EXAMINATION (USMLE)

USMLE test	Exam type	Total duration	No.of Questions	Skills Assessed
Step - 1 (Pass/Fail)	Computer Based	8 hour exam (45 min break time + 15 min optional tutorial)	7 - 60 min Blocks of 40 MCQs, total of 280 questions	Includes pre clinical subjects with biostatistics, behavioural sciences, ethics and public health sciences
Step - 2	Computer Based	9 hour exam (45min break time+ 15 min optional tutorial)	8 - 60 min blocks of up to 40 MCQs, total of no more than 318 questions	Clinical subjects+ biostatistics, behavioural sciences, ethics and public health sciences.
Step - 3 Day 1	Computer Based	7 hours	6 blocks of 30-39 questions each,60 min each block	Foundations of independent practice
Step - 3 Day 2	Computer Based	9 hours	6 blocks of 30 questions each, 45 min per block+ 13 case simulations(10-20 mins per case)	Advanced clinical medicine.

The USMLE is far more than just clearing three steps; it is a comprehensive journey that demands immense patience, resilience, and determination. However, one essential reminder is this: ***It is never too late to pursue this path.***

The ideal timeline suggests taking **Step 1** in your third year of medical school and **Step 2 CK** during your final year or post-internship. However, this is not set in stone. You can tailor your timeline based on your circumstances, preparation, and readiness.

Building a Strong CV

A robust CV is crucial for standing out in residency applications. But how do you craft one? Let's break it down:

1. **Extracurricular Activities**

   Your hobbies are more important than you might think. Unfortunately, many of us abandon our passions in medical school due to the demanding schedule. However, continuing or reviving your hobbies not only enhances your CV but also helps manage stress. Pursuing interests like painting, music, sports, or writing shows that you are a well-rounded individual capable of balancing your personal and professional life.

2. **Research and Publications**

   Research experience and publications are highly valued in residency applications. To get started:
   - ICMR-STS Program: This initiative, available in your second year, is an excellent entry point for research.
   - Seek mentorship from seniors, postgraduates, and professors. They can guide you in selecting topics, conducting research, and publishing papers.
   - During clinical rotations, look for opportunities to write case reports.

3. **Conferences and Competitions**

   Attending medical conferences is both enjoyable and an effective CV-building activity.

   Participate in workshops and competitions such as debates, case presentations, and poster presentations. Networking at conferences can open doors to collaborative opportunities and mentorship.

4. **Volunteering Activities**

   Volunteering adds substantial value to your CV. Whether it's participating in health camps, working with NGOs, or organizing awareness programs, these experiences demonstrate your dedication to serving the community.

5. **United States Clinical Experience (USCE)**

   USCE is a non-negotiable component of a strong CV. It provides hands-on experience in the U.S. healthcare system, including exposure to:
   - **Electronic Medical Records (EMR)**: Understanding and navigating electronic documentation systems.
   - **Medical Insurance**: Gaining insights into the intricacies of the U.S. insurance framework.

- **Networking Opportunities:** Building connections with U.S. physicians and securing Letters of Recommendation (LORs) from them, which are critical for residency applications.

Types of USCE: Electives (Clerkships), Externships, Sub-Internships

Note: Observerships and research electives, while valuable, are not considered USCE.

After completing Steps 1, 2 CK, and 3, there's one additional requirement: the **OET (Occupational English Test)**. This language proficiency test is essential for demonstrating your communication skills and is also required for ECFMG certification.

There is usually a fixed timeline called the **ERAS timeline:**

Year Before Application
- **Jan–June**: Take USMLE Step 1, Step 2 CK; start ECFMG certification (for IMGs).
- **June–Aug**: Register with ERAS, prepare documents (LoRs, personal statement, transcripts).

Residency Application Year
- **July–Sept**: Submit ERAS application (early submission is key).
- **Oct–Jan**: Attend interviews.

Match Process
- **Feb**: Submit Rank Order List (ROL).
- **March**: Match Week (SOAP for unmatched applicants, Match Day results).

Residency Start Year
- **April–June:** Onboard with your program.
- **July**: Begin residency.

If you are an USMLE aspirant, gear up guys it's a long journey ahead, find yourself a good study partner and a mentor, also a puppy to help you with the stress.

Professional and Linguistic Assessments Board (PLAB)

PLAB pathway is designed for international medical graduates (IMGs) who wish to practice medicine in the **United Kingdom**. It assesses whether candidates have the skills and knowledge necessary to work as a doctor in the **UK**. Here's a summary of the PLAB pathway:

Steps in the PLAB Pathway

1. **Meet Eligibility Criteria**

    Primary Medical Qualification (PMQ):

    You must have graduated from a medical school listed in the World Directory of Medical Schools.

    English Proficiency:

    Pass an English language test such as:

    *   **IELTS Academic**: Minimum score of 7.5 overall, with at least 7.0 in each component.
    *   **OET Medicine**: Grade B in each component (reading, writing, speaking, listening).

2. **Register with the GMC (General Medical Council)**
    *   Create an account on the **GMC Online Portal.**
    *   Ensure your documents are ready, including your PMQ, internship completion certificate, and English test results.

3. **PLAB Test**

Test	Format	Content	Duration	Location	Eligibility
PLAB - 1	A written exam with 180 multiple-choice questions (MCQs). Location:	Clinical scenarios reflecting real-life medical practice in the UK.	3 hours	Conducted in various countries worldwide	Must complete IELTS/ OET before applying
PLAB - 2	Objective Structured Clinical Examination (OSCE) with 18 clinical scenarios.	Tests practical skills, including patient communication, diagnosis, and management.	About 3 hours.	Conducted only in the UK	Must have passed PLAB 1 within the last three years

4. **GMC Registration**
    - Once you pass PLAB 1 and PLAB 2, you can apply for provisional or full GMC registration with a license to practice in the UK.
    - Documents required: Proof of PMQ, Proof of English proficiency, and Evidence of internship or clinical experience.

5. **Work as a Doctor in the UK**
    - **Provisional Registration:**
      Allows you to work in supervised posts, such as the UK Foundation Programme (FY1).
    - **Full Registration:**
      Allows you to work in unsupervised roles at FY2 or above, or in specialty training.

Timeline

1. **Step 1**: Prepare and pass IELTS/OET. (1–2 months preparation)
2. **Step 2**: Take PLAB 1. (Typically 3–6 months preparation)
3. **Step 3**: Take PLAB 2. (Requires travel to the UK, typically 3 months preparation)
4. **Step 4**: Apply for GMC registration. (1–2 months processing).

AUSTRALIAN MEDICAL COUNCIL (AMC)

Pathway Options

1. **STANDARD PATHWAY:** For most IMGs seeking general registration.
    Step 1: Pass the AMC MCQ Exam (computer-based test).
    Step 2: Pass the AMC Clinical Exam or Workplace-based Assessment (WBA).
    Step 3: Obtain registration via AHPRA after passing both exams.

2. **SPECIALIST PATHWAY:** For IMGs recognized as specialists in their home country.
    Step1: Apply for specialist recognition through the relevant Australian specialty college.
    Assessment may include interviews or supervised practice before full registration.

Timeline

1. **Credential Verification:** Begin EPIC verification (3–6 months).
2. **AMC Exams (Standard Pathway):**
    a. **MCQ Exam:** Multiple sittings available year-round.
    b. **Clinical Exam:** Typically scheduled post-MCQ; limited availability, so book early.

3. **Registration and Practice:** Apply for provisional or general registration through AHPRA.

DUBAI HEALTH AUTHORITY (DHA)

There has been an increase in the number of Indian medical graduates who are pursuing their residency in Dubai and it has very promising opportunities.

1. **English Proficiency:** Pass an English language test if required:
   a. IELTS: Minimum 6.5 overall.
   b. TOEFL: Minimum 79-80 (internet-based).

2. **Take Licensing Exams**
   You need a medical license to practice or train in Dubai:

   - **DHA Exam:** Dubai Health Authority exam for medical licensing.
     a. Register on the **Sheryan portal**.
     b. Submit documents (MBBS degree, internship certificate, etc.).
     c. Prepare for the test, which includes MCQs based on clinical scenarios.
     d. Pass the exam to qualify for practice or residency training.

3. **Apply for Residency Programs**
   - Residency in Dubai is offered by hospitals and institutions like Dubai Health Authority (DHA) or private healthcare groups.
   - Prepare and submit applications with the following documents:
     a. Medical degree and transcripts.
     b. Valid DHA license.
     c. Personal statement.
     d. Letters of recommendation.

4. **Get a Work Visa**
   - Secure a job or residency training position to obtain sponsorship for a **UAE work visa.**
   - Ensure your documents are attested by the **Ministry of External Affairs (India) and UAE Embassy.**

MEDICAL COUNCIL OF NEW ZEALAND (MCNZ)

To practice medicine in New Zealand, international medical graduates (IMGs) must meet the requirements of the Medical Council of New Zealand (MCNZ). Here is a summary of the pathways:

1. **Competent Authority Pathway:** For IMGs who are already registered and practiced in countries with recognized competent authorities (e.g., Australia, UK, USA, Canada, Ireland).

   - **Eligibility**: MBBS from a recognized institution, internship completed, and clinical experience in a competent authority country.
   - **Steps**:
     a. Apply for registration with the MCNZ.
     b. Undergo an orientation program upon arrival in New Zealand.
     c. Start working under provisional general registration.

2. **NZREX Clinical Pathway:** For IMGs from countries without competent authority recognition.

   - **Eligibility**:
     a. Medical degree listed in the World Directory of Medical Schools.
     b. Internship or equivalent completed.
     c. Pass IELTS/OET:
   - **IELTS**: Overall score of 7.5, with at least 7.0 in each band.
   - **OET**: Minimum grade of B in all components.
   - Pass USMLE Steps 1 and 2 CK or equivalent (PLAB Part 1).
   - **Steps**:
     a. Pass the NZREX Clinical Exam (Objective Structured Clinical Exam).
     b. Secure a supervised position in New Zealand.

3. **Vocational Pathway:** For specialists who wish to practice in a specific area of medicine.

    - **Eligibility**:
        a. Specialist qualifications recognized by the MCNZ.
        b. Evidence of work experience and expertise in the specialty.

    - **Steps**:
        a. Apply for vocational registration.
        b. Undergo an assessment of qualifications and experience.
        c. Work under supervision if required before full registration.

4. **Special Purpose Registration:** For IMGs taking up short-term or specific roles in New Zealand, such as locum positions, research, or postgraduate training.

    - **Eligibility**: MBBS and relevant experience in the specific role.
    - **Steps**:
        a. Apply for temporary registration.
        b. Work under limited conditions for a specified period.

General Steps for All Pathways

1. **Credential Verification**: Use EPIC (Electronic Portfolio of International Credentials) for document verification.
2. **Registration Application:** Apply through the MCNZ online portal.
3. **Visa and Work Permit**: Secure a job offer in New Zealand to obtain a work visa.

Supervised Practice: Most pathways require a period of supervised practice before full registration.

"Here's to strong women. May we know them. May we be them. May we raise them."
— *Amy Rees Anderson*

A SYMPHONY OF STORIES

This poem was woven as a heartfelt tribute to my co-authors, inspired by our shared journey of resilience, passion, and growth.
To the women who walked this path together, breaking barriers and lifting each other up—our voices will echo beyond these pages, leaving a legacy of strength and perseverance.

— By Dr. Yashaswi Guntupalli

From the first step to the final mile,
Each of us walked, through trials and trials.
Sleepless nights, dreams so wide,
We stood together, side by side.

Not just students, not just peers,
But **women in medicine**, facing fears.
Breaking barriers, carving space,
With strength, with fire, with endless grace.

Yashaswi, the spark, who lit the way,
With dreams so vast, she mapped the plan.
Madhulika followed, strong and bright,
Guiding us through the second-year fight.

Darshini painted the third-year scene,
Of ward rounds, cases, and what they mean.
Vijayalakshmi held time in her hands,
Writing of a world no one had planned.

Siri Chandana in the final year's tide,
Fought through the storm and walked with pride.
Vijetha knew the weight interns bear,
Through sleepless nights, through endless care.

Githa wrote of crossroads untold,
Where choices are made, and futures unfold.
Prashasti whispered of battles unseen,
The weight of the mind, the need to be seen.

Bonny brought colors, vibrant and bold,
Painting internship in stories retold.
Sarika, with grace, traced her way,
Through med school's maze, night and day.

Deepthi found freedom, wild and true,
Breaking the chains that once subdued.
Yuva walked the intern's road,
With stories of healing, heavy and bold.

Chaitanya, wise, with a heart so kind,
Wrote of the cases that shaped her mind.
ShriRamya, fierce yet warm inside,
A healer, a poet, a mother, a guide.

Sri Sritha wrote of lessons and love,
Of friendships cherished, a gift from above.
Sreeja, through struggles, through silent cries,
Rose from the ashes, touching the skies.

Sujani, weaving highs and lows,
A journey of fire, a path she chose.
Shrishti, from lands where the oceans meet,
Told of medicine's different beats.

Shruti, with wisdom vast and free,
Spoke of rotations across the sea.
A chorus of voices, strong and true,
A sisterhood in white, painted in hues.

This journey we walked, this story we spun,
From strangers to doctors, from many to one.
A legacy written, in struggle and grace,
A tribute to medicine, time cannot erase.

EPILOGUE

The White Coat and Beyond

We stepped into medical school as students, eager and uncertain, and we left as doctors, forever changed. The journey was far from easy, but every moment—the victories and the struggles—brought us to this point.

Through the sleepless nights, the self-doubt, and the moments of triumph, we learned that being a doctor is more than just knowing medicine—it is about facing humanity in its rawest form. It is about standing strong when others cannot, about listening when words fail, about carrying hope even in the darkest times.

This book is a reflection of that journey—of the laughter, the losses, the lessons. But beyond these pages, our stories continue. New hospitals, new patients, and new challenges await us. Yet one thing remains unchanged: the heart that chose this path.

As we move forward, we wear our white coats not just as doctors, but as humans—ready to heal, to serve, and to grow. Because in the end, medicine is not just about saving lives. It is about touching them. We carry more than just medical knowledge. We carry the voices of our patients, the lessons of our mentors, and the memories of the path we walked together.

This book may be complete, but our journey never truly ends. The white coat does not come with all the answers—it comes with a promise. A promise to learn, to grow, and to serve with empathy. The struggles we faced in medical school will evolve into new challenges, but so will our strength.